Operation Shadowstrike:

An Espionage Thriller

By

Maria Law

Dedication

To my dad, who is no longer with us but is always watching over me. And to my brother, whom I lost to lung cancer at the age of 30. To the only family I have left - my mum and my older brother; your unwavering belief in me has given me the strength to move forward each day.

My dad's strength, even when faced with challenges as a handicapped person, taught me to never give up on life or happiness. His lessons on resilience and courage are the foundation of everything I do.

To my family, especially my mum, the strongest person I know, thank you for your love, patience, and constant encouragement. I owe you everything.

Acknowledgment

I would like to express my heartfelt gratitude to "hexapublishing.co.uk" for bringing this story to life!

I look forward to receiving invaluable feedback from my community of readers and hope for encouragement that will inspire me to continue creating new stories whenever inspiration strikes.

Table of Contents

Chapter One: The Briefing Room

Gunshots echoed in the surroundings; men screamed and grunted, looking to protect themselves from the onslaught of gunfire. Blood, crimson and dark, splattered around the floor.

A hooded man, Alex Kane, crouched in the shadows, his black eyes scanning the dimly lit area with a sharp, calculating gaze. The air was thick with dust, and the silence was disrupted only by the distant drip of water from a leaking pipe. Alex's black hair, slightly disheveled, clung to his forehead as he moved stealthily between rusted machinery and crumbling crates.

The abandoned warehouse was decaying, with beams of moonlight piercing through broken windows, casting eerie patterns on the cracked concrete floor. The air smelled musty and old, with a faint hint of rust. Weeds and vines had started to grow on the walls and through the cracks in the concrete, slowly taking over the space.

Alex's tall, lean frame blended seamlessly into the dark, every muscle in his body coiled and ready to spring into action. His mind raced, evaluating every possible escape route, every potential threat. The scent of rust and old oil filled the air, mingling with the faint, acrid smell of something long since burned.

He paused, listening intently. The faint sound of footsteps echoed in the distance, the enemy drawing closer. Alex's heart pounded, but his expression remained stoic, his eyes narrowing as he planned his next move. He knew this warehouse well, every nook and cranny, every hidden passage. It was his advantage, at least for now.

With a silent breath, he moved again, slipping through the shadows like a phantom, every sense heightened, every nerve on edge. He was an agent, after all, trained for this. As he positioned himself behind a large, rusting pillar, he prepared to face whatever came next, his mind as sharp as the blade he kept hidden at his side.

Alex (thinking): *Those bastards! Just wait till I get my hands on you, Mikhael!*

He glanced around and watched as his team members, Max, Roy, Harry, and Chris, took shelter behind cars and walls right next to a panting Zach, who was tasked with recon of the area. Alex narrowed his eyes, confused. But then, his eyes found the large bullet hole in Zach's right arm.

Alex (thinking): *Shit, we need to take him back before he loses more blood!*

Understanding his leader's concerns, Harry nodded once and sprang into action. Alex sighed, relieved, knowing that Harry would take care of Zach.

Alex (thinking): *How the hell did this happen? We were supposed to meet with the Bianchi's today, so where did Mikhael... Oh! Viktor! He planned all this! Only he knew we would be here; he was the one who snitched on us!*

His eyes caught Chris's, who had his gun pointed at his target, waiting for Alex's orders. Alex looked at the opposite side of the building, glaring at his blond enemy. He waved his hand in the air, and immediately, several gunshots resonated in the ample space. The Black Blood gang was caught off guard, and as they began dropping, Alex's team started emerging from different parts of the warehouse.

Alex (thinking): *Let the show begin!*

Alex ran to the left side and was immediately stopped by a gang member. Before the man could move, Alex kicked him near his torso and punched him. He groaned and came at Alex again. Alex dodged the punch and lunged at him, kicking him in the ribs. Not giving him a chance to retaliate, Alex swiftly pulled out his gun and fired at him.

Alex (thinking): *Great.*

Roy: "Alex, at your back!"

Alex heard Roy shouting, warning him. He turned around and shot at the man.

Max: "Alex!"

Alex started running when he heard Max's voice; the adrenaline rush got him, knowing he had caught the enemy! He could just imagine the different ways he was going to torture him. Alex hated Mikhael, and more than that, he hated Viktor and his cunning schemes. He didn't want more people to die.

Alex (thinking): *This has to end.*

Turning round the corner, he was faced with Mikhael fighting off Max.

Mikhael: "Let me go!"

Mikhael pushed Max off him and ran toward Alex, swinging a knife in his direction.

Alex, taken aback by the sudden act of violence, froze for a second. The blade moved toward him, and on instinct, he ducked. Mikhael's fist whooshed past his head, missing by inches. Without hesitation, Alex lashed out with a swift kick to Mikhael's side. But Mikhael was ready. He caught Alex's foot in mid-air and twisted it sharply. Alex gritted his teeth and spun with the momentum. He brought his other leg up and struck Mikhael square in the chest. The impact sent Mikhael stumbling back. Not giving him another chance, Alex snatched his knife and sliced it across Mikhael's back.

Mikhael screamed in agony as the knife left a deep gash in his back.

Now in control, Alex stabbed Mikhael in the shoulder, twisting the knife to cause as much pain as possible.

Max: "Alex, enough! We need him alive!"

Mikhael screamed again. Mikhael was Viktor's man, the one who ruined Alex's life… His cries were a sweet melody to Alex, and he wanted to hear them repeatedly. Mikhael's screams made Alex remember the screams of his family. He wanted to end him, but he knew Max was right; they needed Mikhael alive to defeat Viktor Volkov.

Picking Mikhael up off the ground, Alex spun him around so he was now face to face with the man who hurt his family. At that point, rage took over once more, and Alex rained punches down on Mikhael, breaking his nose in the process. As blood gushed from his nose, Mikhael lost balance and started to sway. Alex used this opportunity to kick Mikhael in the left kneecap, crushing it.

Alex: "Look who's kneeling now!"

Alex kicked him one last time.

Alex: "You'll pay for what you did!"

Alex nodded at Max, panting and sweating. Moving away from the scene, he watched from the sideline as Max bent down and checked Mikhael's pulse. With a sigh of relief, Max glanced at Alex and nodded.

Alex: "Great."

Alex looked around.

Alex: "Let's clean up!"

***

After the incident three years prior, Alex Kane strayed more toward dark things, colors, and thoughts. There wasn't a single thing about him that had 'light' in it. Ever since his family was snatched away from him, he had been living a hollow life. However,, his life had one purpose - to defeat Viktor Volkov. Nothing mattered to him more than that.

Max: "It's all cleared up, Alex!"

Max walked out of the abandoned building. Following protocol, he put his pistol back in the holster.

Alex: "Where's Mikhael?"

Max: "Our men are putting him inside the van. He's unconscious right now, so at the very least, we won't have to listen to his blabbering."

Alex: "I can't wait to get my hands on him. That bastard made me lose so much in the past few months! He...he...."

Alex couldn't say it; it hurt him to recall those memories.

Alex: "I am not letting him live."

Max: "Calm down, Alex. I know what you're going through, man. But you know that we need him to get information to defeat Viktor. And don't forget Mikhael is *his* man. It will turn into a war if you kill him."

Alex: "Alright."

Alex nodded, trying to calm himself.

Max Rivera's tall, muscular frame made him an imposing figure, but it was his calm demeanor that truly set him apart. Long blonde hair, usually tied back, gleamed faintly in the dim light, and his sharp green eyes missed nothing. Max was a cyber warfare expert with a deep knowledge of computer science and military technology. He always carried his electronic devices with him. However, he wasn't just the brains of the operation; he would often help Alex physically take down the bad guys.

Max didn't speak much or interact, but Alex knew him like the back of his hand. Apart from his brother, Roy, Max wasn't as close to the others as he was to Alex. They shared almost every secret and could understand each other without ever having to say anything.

It could also be said that Alex knew more about his team than they did.

Roy: "Boys!"

Alex started smiling widely when he heard Roy, his very energetic teammate, call out to them.

Max: "Here he comes."

Roy: "I heard you!"

Alex couldn't help but chuckle at them. Even though Max and Roy were twins, they would always bicker with each other. There wasn't anything common between them; instead, they were opposite. While Max was reserved and liked things to be quiet, Roy, on the other hand, was a social butterfly and extroverted.

In contrast to their personalities, Max and Roy shared almost the same features: tall, beautiful green eyes, a beautiful smile, and dimples. The only thing that helped people tell them apart was that Max had long blond hair, and Roy kept his hair short, with a shaved-back-and-sides look.

Alex glanced up and down at Max's black t-shirt and trousers and then at Roy's long blue coat over his turtle neck sweater. Uneasy, he gazed at his attire, which was a grey hoodie and black pants.

Alex (thinking): *I guess everyone can feel who the real fashionista among us is.*

Roy: "Enough of this, please!"

Roy threw his hands up and then looked at Alex.

Roy: "We have already caught the enemy; it's all over now. Don't worry about Zach. Chris took him to the hospital as soon it was over."

Alex nodded.

Max: "It's not over yet. We never know; Viktor's men might still be lurking in the shadows."

Roy: "Oh, don't be a prude, please. Harry and I thoroughly checked the building for any of those pests. No one is here beside us now, so we are good to go for the 'top-secret meeting.'"

Max and Alex: "The what?"

Roy: "I got a call from Ruby. Director Samantha Wright is looking for us."

Alex: "What kind of meeting is it?"

Roy: "Don't know. She said it's confidential."

Alex and Max glanced at each other, already worried.

***

In the heart of Washington DC, inside an intelligence agency headquarters, the atmosphere in the briefing room was thick with tension. The room was high-tech and secure. Its walls were lined with sleek, dark panels that absorbed any stray light. The polished black tile floor reflected the overhead lights in a muted glow, enhancing the room's environment.

At the center of the room was a long, rectangular table made of dark mahogany, its surface clean and devoid of clutter. Around the table were high-backed ergonomic chairs, each equipped with a built-in screen for every team member to access and display information. Above the table, large monitors were mounted on the wall, showcasing real-time maps and data streams related to the mission.

The room was filled with overhead lights with adjustable brightness and focused spotlights that highlighted specific areas, such as the central table and the monitors. The air was cool and crisp, and the only sound that resonated around was the soft hum of the air conditioner or the occasional tapping of keyboards.

Standing at the head of the table, Director Samantha Wright commanded the room with her presence. Tall with a curvy figure, she had striking grey eyes that seemed to pierce through any pretense. Her long brown hair was pulled back into a sleek ponytail, making her strong, angular features emerge. Dressed in a fitted dark suit, she commanded authority.

Samantha: "Listen up, everyone."

Samantha's voice cut through the air. The room fell silent, every agent's attention snapping to her.

Samantha: "We have a very important mission on hand. Viktor Volkov's criminal organization has been spreading chaos and destruction across multiple continents, and it's our duty to dismantle it. We all are familiar with this man; he's dangerous and cunning. He has a large network of resources and connections. We cannot afford to underestimate him."

She took a deep breath, her gaze sweeping across the team and resting on Alex.

Samantha: "Alex, you'll be leading this operation. I trust you with this. I know you want to bring him down just as much as I do."

Her gaze returned to the entire team.

Samantha: "Our objective is clear: expose Viktor Volkov's criminal network at every cost. We must be meticulous and unyielding in our efforts. I hope you all understand the motive behind our mission: ensuring the safety and security of countless lives."

Alex Kane met Samantha's gaze with unwavering resolve. His rugged appearance, chiseled jawline, and intense eyes reflected his eagerness. Samantha's expression softened slightly as she addressed Alex directly.

Samantha: "This mission is extremely dangerous. Viktor poses a threat to national security. I need you to be vigilant, strategic, and prepared for anything."

Alex: "Understood, Director. We won't let you down."

Samantha paused, allowing the weight of her words to sink in.

Samantha: "Do you have any questions before we move forward?"

The room remained silent, the team members absorbed in their thoughts. With a final nod of approval, Samantha concluded the briefing.

Samantha: "Good. Let's prepare for the operation and execute it with precision. We're counting on each of you to bring this mission to a successful conclusion."

***

Once the briefing concluded, the team dispersed to prepare. They all gathered in their department and started working on their task. Like the briefing room, this room was equipped with cubicles for every team member with various electronic devices. Alex glanced at his team and realized one of them was missing.

Alex(thinking): *Zach.*

Alex: "How is Zach now?"

Chris: "He's better. But he still needs to stay under observation for a day as a precaution."

Alex: "I want you all in my office in ten."

Not a minute later, everyone gathered in his office, taking their places around the large table in the center of the room. Coughing slightly, he asked for his team's attention. Next to him, Max Rivera nodded, encouraging him to speak.

Alex's gaze then shifted to Emily Chen. Petite and with striking blue eyes often hidden behind glasses, Emily's long black hair was straight and neatly kept. Her practical attire a simple dark blouse and trousers belied the depth of her analytical skills. She looked nervous but resolute. Alex took a deep breath and addressed his team with a serious tone.

Alex: "Alright, let's break this down. Our mission is to dismantle Viktor Volkov's organization. We need to hit hard and fast."

Alex turned his attention to Max, who sat with a focused expression, his fingers drumming lightly on the table.

Alex: "Max, you'll handle all cyber operations. Viktor's organization works in digital networks, and it's your job to breach their defenses, gather intelligence, and disrupt their operations. Your expertise in cyber warfare will be key to our success."

Next, he looked at Emily, who had been nervously adjusting her glasses.

Alex: "Emily, you will sift through the information we gather, identify patterns, and provide strategic insights. Your ability to make sense of complex data will help guide our actions and keep us one step ahead."

Max and Emily both nodded.

Alex's gaze then moved to Roy, Chris, Harry, and Ruby, who were seated together. Chris was the tactical expert. He was tall and broad-shouldered, with a build that spoke of both strength and agility. His sandy blond hair was cropped short, and he had piercing blue eyes. Harry had a lean build and a mysterious appearance. His short, neatly combed brown hair and glasses gave him a scholarly look, while his focused brown eyes conveyed a sharp intellect. Ruby was petite with a sharp, observant gaze. Her long brown hair was styled in a bun, and she wore a pair of wire-rimmed glasses that gave her an academic appearance.

Alex: "Roy, you'll coordinate our field operations. Your task is to ensure that we're prepared for any situation on the ground and that our field agents are ready to act swiftly and effectively."

Roy: "Noted, boss!"

All mischievous gone now that Roy was in his element.

Alex: "Chris, you'll provide tactical support. Your expertise in strategy and combat readiness will be essential in executing our plans and responding to any threats that arise."

Chris nodded and immediately got to work.

Alex: "Harry, you'll be responsible for securing our communications. We need to ensure that our exchanges remain confidential and protected from interception."

Harry: "On it, boss!"

Finally, Alex looked at Ruby.

Alex: "Ruby, your job is to monitor all surveillance feeds. You'll keep an eye on Viktor's activities and alert us to any suspicious movements or changes in their operations."

Ruby: "Alright, boss."

Ruby nodded.

Alex: "We're dealing with a serious threat, but I trust each of you. This mission is critical, and we need to stay focused and coordinated. Let's execute this operation with precision and make sure Viktor Volkov faces justice."

The team exchanged glances, each of them ready for the mission. As the team began to disperse, Emily lingered behind. She approached Alex with a hesitant smile, her blue eyes searching his face.

Emily: "Alex, I just wanted to say…I know this mission is going to be tough. I'm here to support you, whatever you need."

Alex glanced at her, unaware of her intention or motive.

Alex: "Thanks, Emily. I appreciate the support."

Emily's smile faltered slightly, but she tried to maintain her composure.

Emily: "I'll get started on the data analysis then."

Alex gave her an encouraging nod.

Alex: "Great. I know you'll do an excellent job."

Emily nodded at him once and left the room. With the room now empty, Alex turned his attention to the documents he had laid in front of him. It was the confidential information about Viktor Volkov and his team members.

Alex (thinking): *Today's going to be a long day…*

Alex flipped through the pages and got back to work.

Chapter Two: Unseen Enemies

The dimly lit room reeked of damp concrete and fear. A broad man stood at the center, his sharp eyes scanning the faces of his men who lined the walls, their expressions grim and unreadable. In front of him, on his knees and trembling, was Anton, one of his most trusted lieutenants. The flickering light of a single bulb hanging from the ceiling cast eerie shadows, increasing the tension in the room.

The man, Viktor Volkov, stood tall, a looming figure full of authority. At 33 years old, he had the presence of a man who had seen too much and survived it all. His long black hair was pulled back into a neat ponytail, accentuating the sharp angles of his face. Piercing blue eyes, cold and calculating, seemed to see through the very souls of those who dared to meet his gaze. His muscular frame attested to his years of rigorous training, first as an ex-elite intelligence operative and now as the leader of a vast criminal empire.

Viktor's attire was as sharp as his mind a tailored black suit that hugged his powerful build, contrasting starkly against the white shirt beneath, with his tie perfectly knotted. Everything about him, from how he moved to how he spoke, exuded an air of authority. Viktor's presence dominated the basement. He was a man of few words, preferring action to speaking, and his reputation as a ruthless man was well-earned. Each step he took echoed against the cold floor, a sound that seemed to tighten the grip of fear on everyone present. Anton flinched at the sound, sweat dripping down his forehead despite the chill in the air.

Viktor: "You disappoint me, Anton."

Viktor's voice was low and controlled. It was the voice of a predator, calm yet filled with an underlying threat. The way he spoke, each word carefully measured, was more terrifying than a shout. He pulled a sleek silver knife from his coat pocket, inspecting its blade casually. The room was so silent that the faint sound of metal sliding against leather seemed deafening.

Anton: "I swear, Viktor, I didn't mean to "

Anton stammered, his voice cracking. His hands were bound behind his back, and he could barely keep himself upright as fear sapped his strength. Viktor cut him off with a swift gesture.

Victor: "You think I care about your intentions? You betrayed my trust."

His eyes narrowed, cold blue eyes that felt like they could strip away any defense Anton might try to muster. He knelt down to Anton's level, their faces inches apart.

Victor: "In our world, trust is everything. You knew that when you joined me."

Anton's eyes darted around the room, searching for any sign of mercy, but he found none. The other men remained still, their faces a mask of indifference. They knew better than to intervene; Viktor's word was law, and anyone who crossed him did not live to tell the tale.

Anton: "Please, Viktor…I was trying to protect my family."

Anton was desperate. Tears welled up in his eyes as he realized the gravity of his mistake. But Viktor's expression didn't change.

Viktor: "You had a choice, Anton. You could have come to me. Instead, you chose to sell information to the enemy, thinking you could outsmart me. That was your first and last mistake."

Without another word, Viktor stood and motioned to two of his men. They stepped forward, their faces impassive, and grabbed Anton by the shoulders, dragging him to the center of the room. Anton struggled weakly, his pleas now incoherent with terror. Viktor watched as they secured Anton to a chair, binding him tightly. His men took their time, ensuring that every knot was perfect and that Anton could not move an inch. The air grew thick with tension; everyone feared Viktor's next move. Finally, Viktor approached, the silver knife gleaming in his hand. He looked down at Anton, who was now sobbing uncontrollably.

Viktor: "I want you to understand, Anton. It's not revenge. It's a message for my loving enemy!"

With that, Viktor plunged the knife into Anton's chest with practiced precision, twisting it to maximize the pain. Anton's scream echoed off the walls, a sound of agony that made even the hardened men in the room flinch. Viktor didn't hesitate, delivering another blow, and each one deliberate a lesson to those who might dare to betray him.

When it was over, Viktor wiped the blood off the blade with a handkerchief, his expression unchanged. Anton's lifeless body slumped in the chair, his blood pooling on the floor. Viktor turned to his men, who stood silently, their faces pale.

Viktor: "Let this be a reminder."

Viktor's voice cut through the silence like a blade.

Viktor: "Loyalty is everything. Betray me, and you will suffer the consequences."

With that, he walked out of the room, leaving the men to dispose of the body. The message had been delivered.

***

Viktor Volkov sat in his penthouse office high above the bustling streets of Moscow, the city's lights reflecting off the large, floor-to-ceiling windows behind him. The view was breathtaking, but Viktor paid no mind to it. His focus was entirely on the mission laid out before him. The spacious office, with its sleek, modern design, was the center of his sprawling criminal empire. A large mahogany desk was placed in the center of the room, covered in files, photographs, and a laptop displaying encrypted data streams.

His eyes closed, Viktor leaned back in his chair, his mind carefully sifting through the complexities of his plan. He had no room for error; this operation was too important.

Beneath the surface, Viktor was a man driven by a moral code that he rarely shared with others. He was rebelling against a world he viewed as irreparably corrupt. The agency he once served had betrayed him, and in his eyes, the entire system was rotten to the core. Now, he wielded his power for personal gain and to tear down the structures he believed were oppressing the people.

Yet, his moral code was not one of mercy. Viktor was willing to cross any line and commit any atrocity to achieve his goals. He justified his cruelty with a cold logic: the world was a battlefield, and only the strongest and most cunning would survive. To Viktor, every action he took, no matter how brutal, was a necessary step in his war against the powers that ruled the world. He had long since accepted that sacrifices were inevitable, and he had no qualms about being the one to make them. And those who dared to stand against him would soon learn that there was no room for weakness or betrayal in Viktor's world.

Knock. Knock.

Viktor: "Come in."

The heavy oak doors to Viktor Volkov's office swung open with a soft creak, and Natalia Petrova confidently stepped inside. Her presence commanded attention as she moved with the grace and silence of a shadow. Viktor opened his eyes and looked up at her.

Natalia was a striking figure tall and lean. The tailored suit she wore highlighted her hourglass figure. Her black wavy hair was pulled into a tight braid that hung down her back, each strand perfectly in place. Her brown eyes, deep and unreadable, surveyed the room before settling on Viktor, their usual cool composure betraying nothing of the thoughts running through her mind. She crossed the room, her heels clicking softly against the polished floor, and stopped a few feet from Viktor's desk.

Viktor: "Natalia. I trust you've reviewed the files?"

She nodded, handing him a slim folder with detailed reports and surveillance photos.

Natalia: "Everything is in order. We're ready to proceed as planned."

Viktor took the folder, but his eyes lingered on her for a moment longer than necessary. There was something about Natalia that had always intrigued him. She was more than just his second-in-command; she was his most trusted ally, the one person he could rely on to execute his plans with precision.

As she stood before him, waiting for his next command, Viktor couldn't help but admire how she carried herself every movement calculated, every word measured. But beneath that calm exterior, he knew there was more to her that intrigued and challenged him.

Viktor: "Sit."

He gestured to the chair across from him.

Viktor: "We need to review the details again."

Natalia complied, lowering herself into the chair with the same grace she had entered the room.

Viktor: "I trust you've reviewed the intelligence on the upcoming operation."

Viktor's voice was low. He didn't need to raise his voice to command attention; his presence alone demanded it. Natalia's focus never wavered as she met Viktor's gaze, her mind already running through the plan's details.

Natalia looked up, her green eyes meeting Viktor's blue ones. She nodded, a thin file clasped in her hand. She moved closer and placed the file on the desk between them.

Natalia: "Yes, Viktor. I've gone through everything."

Viktor: "Our objectives are indeed far-reaching. What we're planning is a big moment for me."

Natalia: "I've noted the security measures and potential risks. But the scope of this mission it's unprecedented. What exactly are we preparing for?"

Viktor: "What we're planning will shift everything. It's a move that will solidify our control over the world."

Natalia's brow furrowed slightly, but she kept her expression neutral. She had her doubts, but she knew better than to voice them openly. She couldn't understand why it seemed he was doing all this because of his personal vendetta rather than for the organization. She couldn't help but think that the motive behind this mission was far more dangerous.

Natalia: "You're implying this isn't just about the organization?"

Viktor: "Precisely. This operation will lay the groundwork for me, redefining my power. The details are still unfolding, but I can assure you that its impact will be felt far beyond our usual sphere."

Natalia's thoughts raced as she absorbed Viktor's words.

Natalia: "I'll ensure the team is prepared for every eventuality. But is there anything specific we should be aware of?"

Viktor's eyes flicked to Natalia, his expression inscrutable.

Viktor: "You're confident in your team's ability to execute this?"

Natalia: "Yes. They're the best we have. However, the mission will require more than just skill. We're dealing with powerful enemies, and any misstep could have big consequences."

Viktor nodded.

Viktor: "I trust your judgment, Natalia. If we succeed, it could give us the leverage to control everyone."

There was a brief silence as Viktor's gaze lingered on Natalia. The air between them thickened with unspoken tension, something neither could afford to acknowledge openly.

Victor: "Before we proceed, I need to know if there are any concerns we should consider."

Natalia hesitated for a moment, her thoughts shifting from the mission to the threat.

Natalia: "There is one thing. I've noticed some people have been keeping a tab on us."

Viktor's expression darkened, and his mind went over his list of enemies.

Viktor: "Who?"

Natalia: "Alex Kane and his team."

Viktor's eyes narrowed as soon as he heard Alex's name. Memories of their time together flashed before him memories of friendship, betrayal, and the final fracture that left them on opposite sides.

Now that Alex was involved, Viktor knew the mission was going to be harder, but that was nothing new to him. His entire life had been one high-stakes game after another, each more dangerous than the last. Like all the others, this mission was a risk, and Viktor never played a game he wasn't confident he could win.

Viktor: "Then we proceed. Natalia, you'll lead the team. Take as many people as you want. I'll coordinate with you from here. Inform everyone to pack; you'll leave tonight."

Natalia nodded, her expression serious.

Natalie: "Understood. I'll begin assembling the team immediately. We'll need the best people we can trust."

Viktor: "Trust."

Viktor repeated, a faint smirk playing on his lips.

Viktor: "It's a rare commodity, isn't it? Make sure those you choose understand the stakes. Failure is not an option."

As Natalia gathered the files and prepared to leave, Viktor's gaze lingered on her a moment longer than usual. The room's atmosphere shifted subtly. Viktor leaned back in his chair, a faint smile playing on his lips as his eyes traced the contours of Natalia's face.

Viktor: "Natalia."

His voice was both commanding and intimate.

Viktor: "You've always been invaluable to me. Not just as my second-in-command, but as someone I can rely on in ways I can't with others."

Natalia paused at the door, sensing the change in the air. She turned back to face him, her expression controlled, though she could feel her pulse quickening.

Natalia: "Thank you, Viktor."

Her voice was steady, but there was a guarded edge to her tone.

Natalia: "I've always done what's necessary for our mission."

Viktor stood, moving around the desk with the grace of a predator. He approached her, his tall frame casting a shadow over her as he reached out, his fingers brushing against a loose strand of her hair that had escaped her braid.

Viktor: "You've done more than that."

He gently tucked the strand behind her ear, his hand lingering near her face.

Viktor: "I've come to rely on you in more ways than one, Natalia."

The touch was light, almost tender, but it still troubled her. Natalia hesitated, and for a brief moment, her mind raced with conflicting thoughts. She felt uneasy, but she didn't pull away. She knew Viktor well enough to know what he would do if she avoided his touch. She had spent years controlling her emotions; even in the most precarious situations, she couldn't lose it now.

Natalia: "Viktor, I will do my best for the mission, just like you. That's what matters."

Viktor's blue eyes searched hers as if trying to decipher what lay behind her facade. There was a flicker of something doubt, perhaps but it was gone as quickly as it appeared. He let his hand drop, but the tension hung between them.

Viktor: "Of course. The mission always comes first."

Natalia gave a small, almost faint nod. With that, she turned and left the room, the door closing softly behind her. Viktor watched her go, his expression darkening as he returned to his desk.

***

As soon as Natalia turned into her office's corridor, she let out a breath she didn't realize she had been holding. She leaned back to the wall closest to her and sighed in relief. Her fingers brushed the spot where Viktor's hand had touched her hair, reminding her of the uncomfortable encounter. The coldness of the wall against her back brought another memory rushing to the surface, one she hadn't revisited in years.

It was a cold, gray winter afternoon in Moscow. The streets were slick with ice, and the biting wind cut through Natalia's worn coat as she trudged along the sidewalks, her breath visible in the frigid air. At just twenty years old, Natalia had already faced more hardship than most people twice her age. She was an orphan with no family to turn to and nowhere to go. Desperation drove her from one corner of the city to the next, hoping for a break that never seemed to come.

Natalia's stomach growled with hunger. She knew she couldn't keep going much longer without food or shelter. She glanced at the bleak buildings around her, a harsh reality she was living in. The few people she saw hurried past, their faces blank and focused, oblivious to her pain.

She turned a corner and noticed a man leaning against a sleek black car parked near a small café. He was tall and well-dressed, his dark hair styled neatly, and his blue eyes sharp and intense. He exuded an air of confidence that contrasted sharply with Natalia's appearance.

The man's gaze followed her as she walked by, and he straightened up with a small smile. Weary and wary, Natalia slowed her pace, unsure whether to keep walking or stop. The man pushed himself out of the car and walked toward her.

The man: "Excuse me. You look like you could use a moment of warmth."

Natalia eyed him cautiously.

Natalia: "I don't have any money. I don't need charity."

The man raised an eyebrow, a hint of amusement playing on his lips.

The man: "I'm not here to offer charity. My name is Viktor Volkov. I've been looking for someone with your skills."

Natalia frowned, puzzled.

Natalia: "Skills? I don't have any skills."

Viktor's smile widened slightly.

Viktor: "I think you're selling yourself short. I've noticed your resourcefulness. You've been making your way through this city with a willpower that's rare."

Natalia was skeptical, but something in Viktor's tone and demeanor caught her interest.

Natalia: "Why would you be interested in me?"

Viktor gestured toward the café.

Viktor: "Let's talk inside where it's warmer. I believe I can offer you an opportunity that could change your situation."

Reluctantly, Natalia followed him into the café. Inside, the warmth relieved her, and she sat at a small table near the window. Viktor ordered coffee for both of them and sat across from her. As they talked, Viktor explained that he had been observing her and believed she had potential. He spoke with a charisma that was both captivating and unsettling, outlining a plan where her skills could be put to use in a way that would offer her both financial stability and a new direction in life.

Viktor: "I can offer you a position where your talents will be valued. In return, you will have the chance to build something significant a future."

Natalia listened, intrigued but cautious. Viktor's offer was a lifeline, but she knew better than to trust easily. The world she lived in had taught her to be wary of promises, especially those made by strangers. Still, as Viktor spoke, Natalia could see he was not just offering a job. He was offering a chance at a new life, something she desperately needed. The decision weighed heavily on her, but the allure of escaping her current hardships was tempting.

By the time their discussion ended, Viktor had left her with a choice: accept his offer and step into a new world or continue struggling alone.

Natalia left the café with hope and uncertainty, knowing that her life would change in ways she couldn't fully grasp.

***

To Natalia, Viktor was a lifeline, a way out of her dire situation. She accepted his offer, not fully understanding the complex and dangerous world she was entering. Over time, Viktor gave her a job and a powerful position in his organization. As his second-in-command, Natalia played a crucial role in his operations. She was skilled in infiltration and counterintelligence, which made her invaluable to Viktor. However, as they worked together, the line between mentor and manipulator blurred. Viktor's influence over her grew, and their relationship became more complicated.

Natalia admired Viktor's intelligence and drive, but she also saw his darker side the brutality and manipulation that came with his power. As the years went by, Viktor Volkov's attitude toward her changed. What started as admiration for her skills and hard work slowly turned into an obsession. He had always respected Natalia's abilities and appreciated her dedication to his organization. But soon, his admiration grew into something more troubling.

At first, Viktor's interest was subtle. He gave her more compliments and showed a warmer demeanor. But over time, he began to cross boundaries. His touches became more frequent, and his looks more intense. He would find excuses to be close to her, often making comments that made her uncomfortable. Despite Natalia's efforts to keep things professional, Viktor's obsession continued. He tried to get close to her, making her feel increasingly uneasy. Natalia did her best to avoid private meetings and deflect his comments, focusing on her work while trying to keep her distance.

Viktor's obsession with Natalia made her uncomfortable. She was caught between wanting to do her job well and dealing with Viktor's unwanted advances. It was a difficult and unsettling position for Natalia, and she struggled to maintain her professionalism while managing Viktor's growing fixation.

With a sigh, Natalia pushed herself off the wall and tried to shake off the discomfort from Viktor's touch. She decided to focus on her task to distract herself. However, Natalie couldn't ignore the feeling that the operation was more than just a routine plan it might lead to something much bigger and more dangerous.

As she walked to her office, Natalia tried to put aside her discomfort and concentrate on the mission. She straightened her shoulders, determination hardening her resolve. Yet, in the back of her mind, Viktor's shadow loomed, a constant reminder that in this world, trust was both a currency and a curse. No matter what happened, she wouldn't let herself be derailed. She had come too far to let anything stop her, but the shadows of her past and the uncertainty of her current situation weighed heavily on her.

Chapter Three: Infiltration

The aircraft passed through a dense layer of gray clouds, its wings slashing through the fog as St. Petersburg slowly emerged below. The fog clung to the streets like a blanket, making it difficult to see the city's contours. The city was barely awake. Alex Kane felt a sense of foreboding settle in his chest as the plane's wheels touched the damp runway with a soft bump. The early morning light struggled to break through the fog, establishing everything in muted, gloomy tones. Stepping off the aircraft, the cold, damp air immediately hit Alex, sharp and biting after the controlled climate inside the plane.

With alert and focused eyes, he studied the surroundings, drawing his collar against the chill. It felt strangely far away from the busy rush of the airport, with the sound of rolling bags and weary people's murmurs. The typical noise appeared muted, as though the mist had masked the city and the sounds around them. Each face in the crowd was examined closely as if it were a possible threat, and every look shared between strangers was interpreted as a calculated move. Alex's senses were acutely aware of potential threats, and every instinct was tuned in.

Bright lights flashed above the terminal as Alex and Max Rivera headed toward customs. Max nonchalantly swung a black duffel bag over one shoulder while Alex's palm hovered over the inside of his jacket, where his paperwork was neatly tucked away.

Alex: "Stay sharp."

He muttered these words while barely turning his head toward Max. His voice was low, almost lost in the ambient noise, but the message was clear. They couldn't afford any slip-ups.

With a practiced indifferent attitude, Alex slid his passport and visa over the counter as they neared the customs checkpoint. The man in charge of customs, a severe-looking man with a well-groomed mustache, gave him a fleeting glance before going over the paperwork. There was a noticeable tenseness in the atmosphere, a subtle hint of unease that Alex covered up with a calm demeanor. The officer's eyes flickered up, locking with Alex's for what seemed like an age before he stamped the passport, giving it back to Alex without saying anything.

Max went through the same process, his demeanor equally composed, though Alex could sense the underlying tension. Their passports and identities were flawless, painstakingly crafted by their handlers back in the US. Everything had to be perfect no discrepancies, no questions asked. As they stepped away from the counter, the low murmur of voices and the soft beeping of security scanners faded into the background, replaced by the more pressing concerns of the mission ahead.

As they stepped out of the station and called a cab, the city's cool breeze seemed to follow them. The tires' regular thrum on the damp pavement and the sporadic rattle when they struck a pothole, were the only sounds to be heard throughout the silent trip to the motel. Shrouded in early mist, the streets of St. Petersburg seemed to melt together, tiny passageways disappearing into darkness, drab buildings with peeling paint, and lone humans bunched up against the cold. The cabbie, an elderly guy with a worn face and eyes that betrayed too many early mornings, ignored the two quiet passengers in the back seat and focused on the road.

Alex exchanged a glance with Max, the unspoken understanding between them needing no words. They were both on high alert, their senses attuned to every detail, every potential threat, as the city unfolded around them. As the cab pulled up to the hotel, an old building with a faded sign and a façade that had seen better days, Alex and Max stepped out, their movements precise and deliberate. The driver muttered something in Russian as he returned the change, but Alex only nodded, his mind already elsewhere. The hotel loomed before them, its windows darkened by grime, the entrance lit by a single flickering bulb that cast a sickly yellow glow over the cracked steps.

The door creaked as they walked into the lobby, alerting the drowsy receptionist behind the counter to their presence. The smell of dust and worn carpet saturated the stifling air within, a sharp contrast to the cold outdoors. The young woman at reception, her eyes weary and her smile strained, welcomed them in English with a strong accent before requesting their passports. Giving the documents to her, Alex observed intently as she looked through them, her fingers tapping idly on the computer as she entered their details.

The anxiety of the moment weighed on each second as it passed. Alex's eyes scanned the space, taking note of the aged furniture, the fading wallpaper, and the old-fashioned décor details that, although seemingly unimportant to most people, might provide vital cover in an emergency. He glanced over and mentally noted the location of a security camera whose red light was flashing now and then in the corner. At last, the receptionist gave them both keycards and returned their passports.

Receptionist: "Room 402."

She said with a practiced smile, but her eyes remained flat, betraying her fatigue. Alex and Max nodded, taking the cards and moving toward the elevator without a word.

The elevator ride was slow, the ancient mechanism groaning as it ascended to the fourth floor. The light inside flickered. When the doors finally opened with a jolt, they stepped out into a narrow hallway lined with more faded wallpaper and doors that had seen countless guests come and go. They found their room at the end of the hall, the door's paint chipped and the number barely hanging on. Alex swiped the keycard and pushed the door open, the hinges creaking in protest.

The room was as expected small, with a single window overlooking an alley. The curtains were drawn tightly shut. Two beds with thin mattresses, a small desk cluttered with old magazines, and a television that looked like it hadn't worked in years completed the sparse furnishings.

The mood changed the moment the door closed behind them. All the tension that had been building beneath the surface surfaced. With trained precision, Alex and Max discarded their jackets and quickly gathered their belongings. With a flick of his wrist, Max activated a tiny gadget he had put on the desk a portable signal jammer ensuring that their talk would stay secret. Emily had already taken up her position, her laptop screen illuminating the feeds from the many city surveillance locations she was watching.

Emily: "I've got eyes on the target."

Her voice was calm and professional as her fingers moved deftly across the keyboard, pulling up various data streams and camera angles.

Alex nodded, taking in the layout of their temporary headquarters. The room might have been bland, but for the next few hours, it would serve as the nerve center of their operation.

Alex: "Let's go over the plan one more time."

His voice was low and steady as they gathered around the small city map on the desk.

Max: "The hideout is here."

He pointed to a spot on the map.

Max: "We'll move through these side streets to avoid the main roads and enter the building from the rear. There's less surveillance there, but we'll still need to be careful."

Alex: "Once inside, we stick to the shadows and avoid detection. Emily will guide us through the security systems, but we must be ready for anything. No unnecessary risks."

Alex and Max exchanged a final glance, a quiet declaration of mutual confidence. With one last nod, they started to prepare, their movements focused and precise. Every piece of gear was examined twice, and every detail was considered. With his thoughts already focused on their upcoming assignment, Alex took one last look around the room before they exited. It was time to get started; the planning phase was now complete. Taking a deep breath, they left the relative safety of the hotel room behind and ventured out into the corridor. The main struggles of the day only began for Alex and Max, even though the city outside was starting to wake up.

The thick fog that clung tenaciously to the streets of St. Petersburg made it difficult for the early morning sun to break through. The mist enveloped the city, muffling hues and sounds and transforming the surroundings into a sad, chilly, gray environment. The low-lying fog moved slowly, clinging to the building bases like spectral tendrils and moving down the cobblestones. Occasionally, a little beam of sunshine would try to peek through, only to be quickly engulfed by the dense, impenetrable darkness.

Max Rivera and Alex Kane made their way cautiously and painstakingly through the tiny passageways in silence. In the icy air, every breath they released created tiny clouds that disappeared practically as soon as they materialized. With each misstep, the slippery cobblestones beneath their feet might easily betray them; they gleamed wetly. With his eyes keen and piercing, Max cast a sidelong glance toward Alex, seemingly able to sense the perils lurking ahead through the mist. His breath came in slow, controlled bursts, barely audible above the distant sound of traffic starting to move in the more crowded parts of the city in the early morning.

Alex (whispering): "We're close."

His voice was so low that it blended with the mist.

Alex: "The hideout should be just around the next corner."

Alex took a while to reply. With a predator's precision, he scanned the alley with his dark eyes concentrated on every corner. He felt the old tightness rising in his chest, ready to explode at the first hint of danger like a spring. His thoughts were racing through his head, recalling previous missions testing his mettle. The towering, imposing buildings around them had been neglected for years, leaving their exterior faded and chipped. With their layers of dust and soot from long winters and unrelenting time, the weathered bricks seemed like ancient sentinels.

Slowly, the structure they were approaching became visible, its outline piercing the mist like a silhouette emerging from darkness. It seemed unimpressive at first appearance, simply another abandoned building in a city entirely of them. But it was more than that to the skilled eye. Years of exposure to the harsh elements had left profound wounds behind as the peeling paint twisted away from the ancient masonry. The windows were opaque, like the lifeless eyes of a giant who had long since passed away, either boarded up or heavily grime-coated. A few fading old signs, the letters almost entirely unreadable, clung to the walls like artifacts from long ago, indications of companies that had long since shut down.

Max: "The place is heavily fortified. They've got laser grids, pressure-sensitive floors, biometric scanners… you name it."

Alex's jaw tightened at the mention of the security measures.

Alex: "Then we make sure we don't trigger anything."

They took a step toward each other. They were hiding behind a rusting dumpster, its once bright green paint now a dark mottled jumble of rot and rust, and it looked as though the fog was closing in around them. Max moved with a calm accuracy matched by his steady, controlled breathing. Reaching beneath his jacket, he produced a tiny, sleek black gadget whose matte finish absorbed rather than reflected the low light.

Max: "Lasers first."

He murmured these words as his fingers moved precisely over the device's smooth surface.

As they approached the next checkpoint, Alex pulled out an RFID keycard they had acquired during their reconnaissance, swiping it carefully to bypass the locked door. Max whispered as they approached the next layer of security, which involved multi-factor authentication.

Max: "This one needs both a code and a heartbeat match."

He set up the spoofing device to simulate the necessary biometric data. The heartbeat sensor pulsed in sync with the generated rhythm, allowing them to pass unnoticed.

When he turned it on, a gentle blue light came on, and the screen showed an intricate grid of lines that symbolized the laser security system within the building. Alex maintained a constant stare toward the entryway. The only sounds in the otherwise silent street were the far rustle of leaves from a distant tree and the distant buzz of distant city activity that appeared worlds away. There was an obvious tension between him and Max, an implicit recognition of the risks involved. Error was not an option.

Max: "Lasers down. We can move."

They took meticulous care as they walked up to the entryway. The door in front of them was weighty. The handle felt chilly under Alex's fingers, the steel's coolness piercing his flesh as a clear reminder of the peril they faced beyond. He inhaled sharply, bracing himself for what was ahead, and turned the handle cautiously and slowly. The door creaked softly, opening just enough to let them go in. The inside was completely dark, with the only light coming from tiny fragments that broke through the filthy windows and produced long, unsettling shadows on the ground.

The floor underneath them contrasted sharply with the building's rugged façade, seeming nearly polished. Alex was aware that they needed to exercise caution since the surface had the potential to conceal traps. Every footfall was placed with care to prevent setting off any concealed alarms, and every stride was a calculated risk. Max dropped to one knee, looking over the floor with meticulous care. Pointing out the tiny, nearly undetectable pressure sensors embedded in the smooth surface, his voice was hardly audible above a whisper.

Max: "Pressure sensors. We'll need to keep close to the walls and move slowly."

The hallways were lined with intelligent cameras that moved in a slow, methodical sweep, their sensors alert to even the slightest noise. Alex and Max synchronized their movements with the cameras, only moving when the lenses were pointed away. The air was tense, and every footfall and breath was carefully measured.

Max noted: "These cameras aren't just eyes they're ears too. They can pick up a pin drop."

They remained silent as they continued, the only sounds being the soft hum of the cameras and their careful steps. They pressed against the cold, rough surface of the walls, inching their way forward with deliberate care. The walls were damp, the moisture seeping through from the outside, making them slick. Every movement was intentional, and every glance shared between them was a silent communication of trust and experience. Alex's eyes locked onto the biometric scanner embedded in the wall as they reached the first checkpoint. It was a small, unassuming device, almost easy to overlook, but he knew it was anything but harmless. The scanner's cold, unblinking eye stared back at him, waiting, demanding a fingerprint and retina scan something they didn't have. Max crouched beside the scanner, his tools ready, his movements precise and practiced.

Max: "This will take a minute."

Back at the hotel, Emily watched the feeds with growing unease. The data coming in was precise, but something in the patterns of the guards' movements set off alarm bells in her mind. She leaned closer to the screen, trying to decipher what her instincts were telling her.

Emily: "Alex, something's off. Stay sharp."

Alex (thinking): "We don't have much time."

His eyes narrowed as he scanned the darkness. He could feel the pressure mounting, the seconds ticking away in his mind like a countdown. Max's fingers moved deftly over the scanner, bypassing its protocols with practiced ease. He stretched the seconds into minutes, each feeling more extended than the last. Finally, with a soft click, the scanner's light turned green, indicating the door was unlocked.

Max (smiling to himself): "Got it."

But the smile faded quickly as a low hum filled the hallway. Alex tensed, recognizing the sound immediately footsteps growing louder with each passing second.

Alex (whispering): "We've got company."

They moved quickly, pressing themselves against a large metal cabinet against the wall. The footsteps grew louder and more distinct. Two guards, their heavy boots thudding against the smooth floor, were making their rounds.

Max's (while looking at Alex): "We can't take them both out without raising the alarm."

Alex: "We'll have to be quiet about it."

Alex's grip tightened on the knife hidden in his jacket. As the guards approached, Alex could see their faces grim and focused, their eyes scanning the darkness for any sign of intruders. When the guards were close enough, Alex struck with lightning speed. His knife sliced through the air, its blade catching the light for a brief moment before it plunged into the first guard's throat. The man's eyes widened in shock, a gurgling sound escaping his lips as he crumpled. Max was just as quick, wrapping his arm around the second guard's neck and squeezing until the man's struggles ceased.

Max: "Nice and quiet. Just the way I like it."

They continued down the hallway, their movements even more cautious now. The building seemed to close around them, its walls narrowing as they passed more security measures.

Max: "This place is more secure than we thought. Whoever set this up knew what they were doing."

Alex: "Volkov doesn't leave anything to chance. That's why we need to be perfect."

They both halted when they got to the last door. The massive, reinforced steel barrier stood out sharply from the beaten, weathered walls around it because of its smooth, unmarked surface. This served as the hideout's central hub, where Volkov kept his most private data.

Max: "This one's going to take some time."

Alex: "We can't afford to be caught here."

Max maneuvered past the security tiers with lightning speed and precision with each motion of his hands. The door's locks were an intricate system of mechanical and digital parts that needed to be unlocked using various techniques. Alex watched the security room monitors as Max worked. The skyscraper was displayed from several perspectives on the displays, yet nothing looked out of place.

Nevertheless, he couldn't eliminate the sensation that they were being watched and that a terrible event would happen. At last, the final lock broke with a loud clang. The door slowly opened to reveal a room crammed with cutting-edge machinery. The area was filled with weird shadows produced by the monitors' blue illumination, giving the equipment an almost lifelike appearance.

Max: "This is it. Let's get what we came for."

As they entered the data center, a room crammed with cutting-edge machinery and glowing monitors, Max quickly began downloading the sensitive information onto a secure drive. The tension in the room was palpable as Alex kept a close watch on the door. Once the data transfer was complete, Max pulled out a small device from his backpack a decoy system designed to mimic the data transfer and continue sending false signals.

Max: "This should keep them busy for a while."

Max planted the decoy in place of the original system. As it started its work, flashing a series of fake commands and data logs, they knew it would buy them crucial time to make their escape.

They moved quickly, their actions methodical and precise. Max's fingers flew over the keyboard as he bypassed encryption protocols and firewalls. Alex stood by, his eyes darting between the screens and the door, every sense on high alert. The tension in the room was almost unbearable, a taut wire that could snap at any moment. The faint hum of the computers and the occasional beep as files were transferred were the only sounds that seemed magnified in the silence.

Alex: "How much longer?"

Max didn't look up from the screen.

Max: "A few more seconds."

But those seconds felt like hours. Alex's mind raced with a jumble of worst-case scenarios: What if we missed something? What if this was a trap?

Max: "Done. Let's get out of here."

They returned the way they had come, each step carefully and planned. However, as they approached the door, a slight click sounded in the corridor, signaling the activation of a tripwire that was concealed in the shadows.

Max: "Run!"

They bolted for the exit, the building erupting into chaos behind them. Alarms blared, hidden panels in the walls slid open, revealing armed guards who poured into the hallway, weapons drawn and ready to fire.

Alex (yelling): "Keep moving!"

As they rounded a corner, Alex spotted a hidden lever embedded in the wall part of their contingency plan. Pulling it down, a section of the wall slid open to reveal a hidden passage.

Alex: "This way!"

The narrow, dark tunnel led them away from the main corridors, allowing them to avoid direct confrontation with the guards. As they emerged from the passage into a back alley, they blended into the early morning fog, making their retreat strategic and undetected. They ran through the little streets. The city that had been a quiet collaborator in their invasion had become an adversary, hiding threats around every corner with its winding streets. Alex heard the thud of boots hitting the pavement and the guards yelling behind them.

Max: "We've got to split up! We'll meet at the rendezvous point!"

Alex nods and turns down a side street, leaving Max on his path. As he ran, his instincts focused on survival, his thoughts racing. Gray and brown blurred the streets of St. Petersburg, the ancient buildings standing like rocks on either side of him. He surged past a cluster of onlookers, his movements so swift that their shocked shouts were hardly audible. The broad avenue he stood on was mostly empty since the early hour had kept most people indoors. He ducked inside the tiny café he saw next to a small alley, his feet banging against the cold, hard concrete.

The walls on each side of the lane were slippery and wet, small and gloomy. Pressing against the wall to gather his breath, he could feel the uneven brick texture beneath his fingertips.

At last, he emerged from the alley, and the noises of pursuit faded into the distance, making the city appear peaceful. He looked at his watch and noted the hour. Even though he was getting near the meeting spot, each step he took felt like it might be his last. Max awaited Alex at the agreed-upon meeting place, a modest, inconspicuous plaza with a few seats and a fountain. His face was pale and drawn, and he breathed shallowly and quickly as he leaned against a brick wall.

Max: "That was too close."

Alex took the drive from Max, feeling its weight in his hand. It was small, almost insignificant, but he knew what contained could change everything.

Alex: "But we made it. "Let's hope what we found was worth it."

Max looked at Alex, his expression serious.

Max: "It better be. We've stirred up a hornet's nest, and they will come looking for us."

Alex's eyes hardened: "Then we'd better be gone before they find us."

They walked swiftly, assimilating into the pedestrian traffic. The city was awakening around them, with people moving through the streets and going about their regular lives without considering the dangers beneath the surface.

Alex: "We're going to need that bond. Because the real fight is just beginning."

Alex thought as they walked, the sun finally breaking through the clouds above.

By the time they arrived at the hotel, the day they had begun. While the surrounding city was bustling with activity, Alex's mind was already on what to do next. They had made a significant discovery that would tilt the scales in their favor. However, new challenges and perils that would put them to the test in ways they could not have predicted arrived with that discovery. The sounds of the city subsided as they approached the hotel, giving way to the lobby's calm, rather clinical ambiance. For Alex and Max, however, the strain persisted. It was always there, reminding them of their high stakes.

Alex paused at the door to their room, his hand resting on the handle. He could feel the weight of the day pressing down on him, the exhaustion setting in. But there was no time for rest. Not yet.

Alex: "We've got work to do."

Max: "Let's get to it."

Max's response was just as quiet but filled with determination.

They stepped inside, the door closing softly behind them, momentarily shutting out the world. But the mission, the dangers, and the challenges ahead were far from over.

Chapter Four: Digital Warfare

Alex and Max wasted no time; the stakes were too high. The hideout mission had succeeded, but the real challenge was beginning. Max immediately moved to the small desk in the corner, setting up his laptop. The mission was far from over, and they both knew that every second counted.

Alex: "Emily, we're back."

He said this is speaking into the secure line. He knew she was monitoring from the hotel, her eyes on the surveillance feeds across the city.

Alex: "Anything unusual?"

Emily's voice crackled through the earpiece.

Emily: "Nothing yet. I've got the feeds up, and everything looks clear, but we should be on alert."

Max didn't wait for further instructions. He powered up the laptop, the screen springing to life with the data they had retrieved. His fingers flew across the keyboard, navigating through the complex layers of encrypted files. Alex stood behind him, his focus sharp, as they delved deeper into Volkov's network.

Max: "The data is extensive."

He said this while his eyes were fixed on the screen.

Max: "Volkov's setup is more sophisticated than we thought. Multiple layers of encryption, adaptive firewalls… it's all designed to keep intruders out."

Alex: "We expected this. Focus on breaching the defenses first. We need to see what he's planning."

Max's fingers moved with practiced precision, bypassing initial firewalls and security measures. The tension in the room was evident, but none of them let it bother them. They'd done it before, but the stakes had never been so high.

Max: "Got through the first layer. There's more, though. This is going to take time."

Alex: "Do what you can. We're not leaving until we have what we need."

As Max continued his work, Alex reached out to Emily again.

Alex: "Keep an eye on the back channels. If Volkov's men get wind of what we're doing, they'll try to shut us down."

Emily: "I'm already on it. There has been no movement yet, but I'll let you know the second anything changes."

Max encountered another more advanced firewall. He moved closer to the screen, his fingers lingering over the keys as he weighed his alternatives. This wasn't simply a breach; Volkov's system was adaptive, learning from each effort to break it.

Max (muttering): "This one's different. It's designed to counter every move we make."

Alex: "Then we need to outthink it. Use the secondary protocols we discussed."

Max nodded, switching tactics. He opened a secondary toolkit, launching a simultaneous attack on the firewall from multiple angles. The screen flickered as the algorithms went to work, and for a moment, it seemed like the system might hold. But then, slowly, the defenses began to crack.

Max: "We're in."

He announced, his voice edged with triumph.

Max (continuing): "But this is just the beginning. There's a lot more to get through."

Alex: "Focus on the most critical data first. Anything that relates to New York or large-scale infrastructure."

Max nodded, his eyes scanning the streams of data now accessible. It was a vast network, and finding the critical information was like searching for a needle in a haystack.

Max: "Wait… here it is. Volkov's planning something big an attack on New York's power grids, communication networks, and public infrastructure. It's a coordinated assault designed to cause maximum disruption."

Alex: "How soon?"

Max: "Hard to say. But it's already in motion. We need to act fast."

Alex: "Get as much as you can. We need to understand the full scope of this plan."

As Max continued to dig deeper, the tension in the room increased. Their uncovered data painted a grim picture Volkov wasn't just targeting a single system. He was going after everything, aiming to bring the city to its knees.

Alex: "Emily, we've got a problem."

Alex said, his voice urgent as he relayed the information.

Alex (continuing): "Volkov's planning an attack on New York. We need to start working on a counter-strategy immediately."

Emily: "Understood. I'll start pulling the resources we need. We can't afford to miss anything."

Max's hands flew across the keyboard, bypassing another layer of encryption. Suddenly, the screen displayed a series of highly encrypted files more complex than anything they had encountered.

Max: "These files are different. There's something buried deep in here that Volkov wanted to hide at all costs."

Alex: "Can you crack it?"

Alex's voice was heavy and tense at this point.

Max: "I'll try. "But it's going to take time."

As Max worked, the atmosphere grew more intense. The minutes he was ticked by, each one bringing them closer to the point of no return. Max's face was a mask of concentration, his eyes fixed on the screen as he tried to break through the final barrier.

Max: "Got it. This is it the final piece of Volkov's plan. He's not just targeting the infrastructure. He's planning to release a virus that will cripple the city's emergency response systems. If it goes through, New York will be completely vulnerable."

Alex felt a chill run down his spine.

Alex: "We need to stop this. Now."

Max nodded, already moving to implement countermeasures.

Max: "I can disrupt the virus, but it will be tricky. If I'm off even a fraction, it could trigger a secondary attack."

Alex: "Do whatever it takes. We can't let this happen."

The following several hours were a blur of frenetic activity. Max worked diligently, his focus unwavering as he passed the mazes of Volkov's digital barriers. Alex remained close, watching every action and ready to intervene when Max needed him. Finally, as the night progressed, Max sat back in his chair, tiredness visible on his face.

Max: "I've neutralized the virus. The immediate threat is contained, but Volkov's network is still active. We've bought ourselves some time, but this isn't over."

Alex nodded, his mind already moving to the next step.

Alex: "We need to keep the pressure on. Emily, stay on high alert. If Volkov makes a move, we need to be ready."

Emily: "Understood."

Max began organizing the data they had retrieved, his hands moving more slowly now, fatigue setting in.

Max: "There's still more we can use here. We must go through it all, piece by piece, to see what else Volkov is planning."

Alex: "We'll do that. But first, let's make sure the immediate threat is completely neutralized. We can't afford any mistakes."

Max nodded, his eyes heavy with exhaustion but still focused.

Max: "I'll start on the analysis. We need to make sure there are no loose ends."

As Max began sorting through the remaining data, Alex turned his attention to the next phase of their mission. They had managed to avert disaster for now, but Volkov was still out there, and the danger was far from over.

Alex: "Emily, stay connected with our contacts in New York. We must coordinate with them to ensure the city is prepared for residual threats."

Emily: "I'm on it. I'll make sure they're updated on everything we've found."

***

A low, steady thrum of equipment could be heard in a location free of metropolitan distractions. The perfume of burning metal and electronic components, with a faint whiff of cigar smoke in the background, lay heavy in the air. A man was spotted standing close to a large screen, his back to the entrance. The light from the monitors cast long shadows on the concrete walls outside the room.

Viktor Volkov looked carefully at the live streams on the television, absorbing every detail. His fingers were tapping against the armrest of his chair in a repetitive pattern. The encrypted data on his screen had the power to knock a nation to its knees and devastate a city, and Volkov relished the prospect of doing so.

As he scrolled through the data streams, he couldn't help but smile, pulling at the corners of his lips. While putting his ideas into reality, each component fell into place with the precision of a well-oiled machine. Volkov knew that Kane and his team were trying to stop him, but he had prepared for the eventuality. His technique consisted of predicting their every move and placing traps inside traps. This was done to ensure that even if they successfully revealed a piece of his plan, they would never be able to complete the mission.

Volkov was viewing a particular stream when he saw a minor blip on one of his monitors. This indicated that someone had penetrated one of his external protections, and it caused his eyes to constrict. He leaned forward slightly to look at the feed, and his fingers stopped moving.

Volkov: "Ah, Kane. I knew you'd find your way here eventually."

His voice was low, more for himself than anybody else. He grabbed a little remote on his desk and pressed a button, which displayed a sequence of orders on the screen. With a few rapid inputs, he initiated a countermeasure a digital trap that would lure Kane's crew deeper into his web, creating the idea of progress while tightening the noose around their necks.

Volkov: "Let's see how far you can get before I tighten the rope."

He leaned back in his chair, watching with a predatory gaze as the feeds flickered and shifted. The game was beginning, and Volkov was ready to play.

***

As the first light of dawn began to break, Alex and Max continued their work, the weight of their task pressing down on them. They had thwarted Volkov's immediate plans, but the battle was far from over.

Alex: "Max, take a break. You've done more than enough for now."

Max shook his head.

Max: "No time for that. We need to stay ahead of this. Volkov isn't going to stop, and neither can we."

Alex placed a hand on Max's shoulder, offering a rare moment of camaraderie.

Alex: "We'll get through this. We've come too far to let Volkov win now."

Max nodded, his resolve unwavering despite the exhaustion.

Max: "Let's finish this."

Alex couldn't quit thinking about the people whose lives hinged on him reaching for his phone. Although the residents of New York were unaware of the threat lurking over them, it was up to him and his squad to prevent Volkov's plan from being carried out.

The clock was ticking, and they had no time to waste.

Chapter Five: Close Call

The early light filtered through the drapes, creating a soft glow over the room. Alex understood they had bought time by defeating Volkov's immediate objectives, but the threat remained looming over New York. Every passing second seemed like a countdown to something bigger something they needed to stop.

Alex: "Max, seriously. You need rest. You can't keep going like this."

Max looked at Alex, his eyes bloodshot but determined.

Max: "I know. But what if we miss something? What if there's another layer we haven't uncovered yet?"

Alex sighed, understanding the weight Max carried.

Alex: "We'll take shifts. I'll dig through the rest of the data while you rest. We need to be sharp for whatever comes next."

Max hesitated but finally nodded.

Max: "Alright, just a couple of hours. Wake me if anything comes up."

Alex watched Max leave his workstation and lie on the improvised bed in the corner of the room. Max was right they couldn't afford to miss anything, but they also couldn't afford to collapse from exhaustion.

Alex sat back down at his laptop, scanning through the remaining files. His mind raced, replaying the events from the last several hours. They had barely scratched the surface of Volkov's enterprise, and there was still so much to uncover. For now, they had a brief moment of calm a pause in the storm.

Emily's voice broke the silence, crackling through the secure line.

Emily: "Alex, any updates on your end?"

Alex glanced at Max, who was already drifting off to sleep.

Alex: "Max is getting some rest. I'm going through the data. How's it looking on your side?"

Emily: "Quiet. Almost too quiet. I've got eyes on all major networks, but there's no sign of movement from Volkov's people."

Alex rubbed his temples, the weight of the mission pressing down on him.

Alex: "Keep monitoring. If Volkov's as smart as we think, he'll be planning his next move already."

Emily: "I will. And Alex… don't forget to take care of yourself too."

Alex managed a faint smile.

Alex: "I'll be fine. We all will be. We need to stay focused."

He ended the conversation and returned his attention to the laptop. The calm in the room was almost oppressive, a sharp contrast to the chaos that had erupted earlier. But Alex knew he couldn't afford to let his guard down. Not now, not when they were this close. Hours passed, and the sun was fully up when Max awoke from his nap. He sat up and rubbed his eyes before stretching his tense muscles.

Max: "How long was I out?"

Alex: "Long enough. Feeling any better?"

Max nodded, though fatigue still lingered in his expression.

Max: "A bit. Did you find anything?"

Alex: "Nothing concrete. It's like Volkov's gone dark. But we both know he's just biding his time."

Max sighed, frustration seeping into his voice.

Max: "He's always one step ahead. It's infuriating."

Alex: "We'll catch up. We have to."

Another call came in from Emily.

Emily: "I've been monitoring everything, but it's quiet. Too quiet. I don't like it."

Alex: "It's the calm before the storm. We need to be ready."

Max stood up, grabbing his laptop.

Max: "I'll set up another sweep. If there's anything out there, we'll find it."

Emily: "I've also been thinking... We should have a backup plan. If Volkov's planning something bigger, we need contingencies."

Alex nodded.

Alex: "Agreed. We can't afford to be caught off guard."

The three of them went over the specifics repeatedly, refining their plans and verifying every angle and possibility twice. The stress rose minute by minute as the hours passed.

Finally, Emily broke the silence.

Emily: "What if we're missing something? Something right in front of us?"

Alex looked at her, considering her words.

Alex: "What do you mean?"

Emily: "Volkov's been playing this game much longer than we have. What if everything we've found so far is... a distraction? A way to keep us busy while he prepares his real move?"

Max frowned, his fingers pausing on the keyboard.

Max: "It's possible. But how do we figure out what the real plan is?"

Emily: "We need to think like him. If we were Volkov, where would we strike? What would be the most effective way to cripple us without us seeing it coming?"

The room fell silent again as they each contemplated the possibilities.

Alex: "We must consider every option, no matter how far-fetched. Emily, keep digging into the data. Max, you keep monitoring the networks. I'll coordinate with our contacts on the ground. We need to be ready for anything."

They all set to work, and the calm resolve in the room was evident. Hours passed as the sun rose higher in the sky. But they didn't stop or relax. There was too much at risk.

As the afternoon progressed, Alex walked outside briefly to clear his mind. The streets were silent, the noise and activity of the city drowned out by the weight of the mission. He strolled a few blocks, his mind cluttered with plans and possibilities. But that old, uncomfortable feeling returned as he proceeded through the quiet neighborhoods. A prickling sensation at the back of his neck warned him that he wasn't alone.

Alex halted, his instincts heightened. He discreetly studied his surroundings, but there was no one in sight. Yet the feeling persisted. His heartbeat quickened, and he knew better than to ignore it.

Alex: "Just a quick walk to clear my head… should've known better."

Muttering to himself, he continued at a steady but vigilant pace. He slowly changed direction without altering his route, guiding himself into a narrower, quieter street. This calculated move would allow him to meet his pursuers on his terms.

The footsteps behind him intensified as he turned the corner into a tight alley. Alex's hand instinctively moved toward the gun hidden inside his jacket as his body tensed. The adrenaline coursing through him sharpened his senses, making every sound and movement more intense.

Alex sensed it was time for a confrontation as the person behind him drew closer. He spun around, prepared to meet his assailant. The figure rushed at him, but Alex's body moved with fluid precision a result of years of battle expertise. He deflected the attacker's punch with a powerful kick to the stomach, causing the figure to stagger back.

Attacker: "You're fast," the figure growled, recovering quickly.

Alex: "You'll have to do better than that."

The attacker regained their footing and drew a knife with a swift motion. The blade caught the light as it approached Alex, but he was faster. He sidestepped to evade the strike, then disarmed the attacker with a precise blow.

The weapon clattered to the ground, but the fight wasn't over. The assailant launched a series of rapid punches. Alex's training took over; he moved with calculated control, dodging strikes and waiting for the perfect moment to counterattack.

Alex: "You're good, but not good enough."

The attacker's frustration mounted, their blows becoming more erratic. Alex seized the opportunity, doubling his strikes and delivering a powerful blow to the attacker's midsection. He twisted the assailant's arm behind their back and shoved them into the wall.

Even after the fight was over, Alex remained on high alert. He kept a firm grip on the attacker and forced them against the wall.

Alex: "Who sent you?"

The only response was a muffled groan. Alex noticed something glinting on the attacker's wrist: a tattoo. Recognition jolted through him this was no random attack.

Without hesitation, Alex ripped the hood off the figure's head, revealing a shock of black hair and piercing eyes. The face staring back at him was all too familiar.

Alex: "Natalia."

Natalia: "Surprised to see me, Kane?"

Natalia smirked, her voice smooth and laced with danger.

Alex: "So Volkov sends his best after me. I'm flattered."

Natalia chuckled, a low, menacing sound.

Natalia: "He knows you're getting too close. Thought I'd deliver a message."

Alex's eyes narrowed, his voice tinged with sarcasm.

Alex: "And what's the message? That he's scared?"

Her smile faded, replaced by a cold, calculating look.

Natalia: "You wish. You and your little team are out of your league, Kane. But you already know that, don't you? Otherwise, you wouldn't be chasing ghosts."

Her remarks struck a nerve, challenging Alex. He scrutinized her face for any signs of weakness, but she revealed nothing. Then, he noticed something partially hidden by her sleeve was the same tattoo he had seen earlier. A cold realization hit him like a punch to the gut. It was the same mark connected to his sister's murder.

Alex: "Where did you get that tattoo?" Alex's voice was low, his anger barely contained.

Natalia's eyes flicked down to her wrist, then back up to Alex with a hint of amusement.

Natalia: "This old thing? It's just a reminder. A reminder of how deep this game goes, Kane. You have no idea what you're up against."

Alex's patience was wearing thin.

Alex: "Try me."

Natalia smirked, her eyes flashing with a dangerous light.

Natalia: "Oh, I will. But not tonight."

Before Alex could respond, Natalia twisted out of his grip with surprising speed, her movements fluid and precise like a seasoned dancer in a deadly routine. Alex's instincts kicked in, and he bolted after her, his pulse pounding with the thrill and urgency of the chase. His eyes strained to keep track of her as she slipped around a corner, her silhouette flickering in and out of view like a ghost. He pushed himself harder, his legs pumping as he closed the gap between them.

But Natalia was too quick, her agility unmatched. She vaulted over a low fence with the ease of someone who had done it a hundred times before, her body twisting mid-air before landing silently on the other side. Without hesitation, she sprinted through a narrow gap between two buildings, disappearing from Alex's line of sight.

Undeterred, Alex followed, his breath coming in ragged gasps. The alleyways twisted and turned, a labyrinthine maze of brick and mortar that seemed to conspire against him. Natalia's figure reappeared ahead of him for a brief moment as she darted across an open courtyard, her head turning slightly as if to ensure he was still in pursuit. A taunting smile played on her lips, visible even in the dim light.

She took a sharp turn, slipping into a narrower alley that was barely wide enough for a person to navigate. Alex cursed under his breath but pressed on, squeezing through the tight space. His shoulder brushed against the rough brick walls, slowing him down just enough for Natalia to widen the distance between them.

Emerging on the other side, Alex caught sight of her again as she dashed across a busy street, weaving between honking cars with the ease of someone accustomed to navigating chaos. The city lights cast long shadows on the pavement, momentarily obscuring her from view. Alex hesitated for a split second, then bolted after her, narrowly avoiding a speeding taxi as he crossed the road.

He could feel the burn in his lungs, the relentless pace taking its toll, but he pushed it aside. The memory of his sister, the sight of that damned tattoo, and the sting of Natalia's taunts all fueled his determination. He couldn't let her get away not when he was this close.

Sensing the chase was nearing its end, Natalia glanced over her shoulder. Her eyes locked with Alex's for a brief moment, and she flashed him a knowing look a mixture of defiance and something that almost resembled respect. Then, with one final burst of speed, she rounded another corner and slipped into an even darker, more secluded alley.

Alex turned the corner, only to be met with empty darkness. The alley was a dead end, with towering walls on three sides and no sign of Natalia. He skidded to a halt, his breath heavy with exertion and frustration. The echoes of the city surrounded him, but there was no trace of her no shadow, no sound. It was as if she had vanished into thin air.

He stood there for a moment, hands on his knees as he tried to catch his breath, the cold night air biting at his skin. He knew he had lost her, but the chase had left him with more than just exhaustion. The tattoo on Natalia's wrist was burned into his mind. That mark, a symbol that had haunted him since Sarah's death, had now resurfaced in the most chilling way. Alex felt the familiar ache of loss, the unresolved grief that had driven him for so long. His sister's memory was always with him, a constant reminder of the life that had been ripped away. But now, with Natalia's revelation, the pain was sharper, more immediate. He couldn't afford to lose focus, not when the stakes were this high.

When Alex returned to the motel, adrenaline still pumped through his veins. His thoughts were a tangled mess of what had just transpired. The takeaway bags he had dropped earlier lay forgotten on the floor. As he entered, Max and Emily looked up; their expressions shifted from concern to alarm.

Max: "Alex, what the hell happened?" Max's voice was tight with worry.

Alex didn't answer immediately. He moved to the window, his mind racing. Memories of his sister, the pain of her loss, the unresolved anger it all came flooding back.

Emily: "Alex?"

Emily's voice was soft but insistent, pulling him back to the present. He turned to face them, his expression grim.

Alex: "I was attacked. It was Natalia."

Emily's eyes widened in recognition.

Emily: "Volkov's second-in-command? What was she doing here?"

Alex: "Sending a message." Alex's voice was tight with controlled fury.

Alex: "But it's more than that. She had the tattoo… the same one linked to Sarah."

Max's voice was quiet, filled with apprehension.

Max: "So this is personal now."

Alex nodded, his jaw clenched with barely restrained rage.

Alex: "It's always been personal. But now… now it's war."

Emily's voice was steady despite the tension in the room.

Emily: "What do we do next?"

Alex took a deep breath, forcing himself to focus. The encounter had shaken him, but it had also steeled his resolve. Volkov had made a mistake he had underestimated just how far Alex was willing to go.

Alex: "We keep going. We dig deeper, find out what Volkov is planning, and take him down. No more games."

Max nodded, his expression hardening with determination.

Max: "We're with you, Alex. Whatever it takes."

Emily: "We'll figure this out. Together."

Alex met their gazes, feeling a surge of gratitude. This team was more than just colleagues they were his family now. But with that trust came responsibility. He couldn't let them down.

Max was the first to break the silence.

Max: "If Natalia's involved, we need to consider that Volkov might be onto our plans sooner than we thought."

Alex: "We need to accelerate our timeline. Whatever Volkov is planning, it's bigger than we anticipated."

Emily: "What about Natalia? She's no ordinary operative. We must be prepared for her to strike again, and she won't make the same mistake twice."

Alex: "We'll have to split our focus. One part of the team digs deeper into Volkov's operations while the other prepares to counter Natalia. We need to anticipate her moves, not just react to them."

Max: "I'll start by analyzing the recent data we've gathered. There might be something we missed that could give us an edge."

Emily: "I'll handle the logistics. We need to secure our location and ensure no one can track us. If Natalia found you tonight, our cover isn't as solid as we thought."

Alex watched them both and felt a deep sense of gratitude. In a world that had taken so much from him, this team was more than just colleagues they were his family. But along with that trust came an obligation. He could not allow them to fail.

The crew worked in tense silence as the evening dragged on. The weight of their mission pressed down on them, knowing they were up against one of the most dangerous criminals in the world and his equally lethal second-in-command. Every decision felt like it could tip the scales between success and failure. Max suddenly broke the silence.

Max: "I found something."

He turned the screen toward Alex and Emily, revealing a map of interconnected lines and points.

Max: "It's a pattern. Volkov's operations are more widespread than we thought, and they're all converging on a single location."

Alex leaned in, studying the map.

Alex: "What's the target?"

Max: "We're still piecing it together, but he's planning something big. A shipment, maybe. Or a meeting with high-level contacts. Whatever it is, it's happening soon."

Emily: "This could be our chance to strike. If we can intercept whatever Volkov is planning, we could cripple his entire operation."

Alex's voice was laced with determination.

Alex: "We'll need to move fast. Natalia will be watching, and Volkov won't be far behind. But if we can pull this off... it could be the break we need."

Max: "I'll keep digging. There has to be more. We can set a trap if we can pinpoint the exact location and time."

Emily: "I'll coordinate with our contacts. We need eyes on the ground and people we can trust. This has to be airtight; there is no room for error."

Alex stepped back, watching as his team moved into action. Despite the tension, there was a sense of purpose a determination to see this through, no matter the risks. But beneath it all, Alex couldn't shake the image of

Natalia's mocking smile, the tattoo on her wrist, and the way she had slipped through his fingers.

As the hours passed, Alex found himself alone again, standing by the window. The city lights stretched before him, a sea of twinkling points in the darkness. But his thoughts were elsewhere lost in memories of his sister, of the life they had shared before everything had been torn apart.

He knew what he had to do. Volkov had taken everything from him, and now it was time to take it back. He wouldn't rest until Volkov and Natalia were brought down until justice was served for Sarah and all the others who had suffered because of them.

Alex: "This ends with us."

He whispered to the empty room, a vow as much as a promise.

Alex: "No matter the cost."

Chapter Six: The Mole

Alex and Max sat in the hotel room, their silence filled with the unspoken weight of the night's events. Natalia's escape, the tattoo that haunted Alex's thoughts, circled in their minds, creating a heavy atmosphere. They were exhausted, but the rest was out of the question. There was too much at stake.

Max: "You think Natalia's gone for good this time?"

Alex shook his head, replaying the confrontation in his mind.

Alex: "No. She'll be back. It's what she does always lurking, always a step ahead."

Max nodded, though the worry lines carved on his face deepened. He glanced at the laptop on the table.

Max: "Samantha should be dialing in soon. We need to debrief and figure out what's next."

Before Alex could respond, a knock on the door pulled both men from their thoughts. Alex's hand instinctively moved to the gun at his side, ready for anything. But when the door opened, it was Emily who stepped inside. Though surprised, her presence brought a mix of emotions for which neither man was prepared.

Alex: "Emily?"

Max stood, just as surprised.

Max: "We weren't expecting you."

Emily's eyes briefly met Alex's before she looked away, her expression guarded.

Emily: "I needed to be here. After what happened, I couldn't stay away."

Alex closed the door behind her, and a small part of him was relieved she was there.

Alex: "You didn't have to come in person."

Emily gave a small, almost nervous smile.

Emily: "I know, but I wanted to. Besides, I've got some updates."

Max pointed to the laptop.

Max: "Samantha's about to call in."

The screen flickered to life as if on cue, revealing Samantha Wright's sharp features. Her grey eyes scanned the room, taking in each with a discerning gaze.

Samantha: "Alex. Max. Emily."

Her tone was brisk and professional, but her concern for her team was unmistakable.

Alex: "Samantha, we need to talk."

Samantha's expression shifted slightly, and unease flickered over her features.

Samantha: "I heard about Natalia. Tell me everything."

Alex took a deep breath, recounting the confrontation in detail. The way Natalia had outmaneuvered him, the fight, and most importantly, the tattoo that had shaken him to his core. His voice remained steady, but there was no mistaking the turmoil beneath the surface. When he finished, Samantha leaned back slightly, her gaze shifting to Emily, who had moved to stand by the window, her arms crossed.

Samantha: "And this tattoo you're certain it's connected to your sister?"

Alex nodded, his hands clenched into fists at his sides.

Alex: "It's the same mark. I've been chasing it for years, and now it's back."

Samantha: "We'll investigate further. This connection could be the key to unraveling Volkov's entire operation."

Max, who had been listening in silence, finally spoke up, his voice laced with concern.

Max: "And Natalia? She's not just another operative. If she's this involved, we need to rethink our strategy."

Samantha: "Natalia's a significant player. We need to be on high alert. She won't make the same mistake twice."

Emily shifted, drawing Samantha's attention.

Samantha: "Emily, you seem distracted. Is there something on your mind?"

Emily forced a smile, shaking her head.

Emily: "No, just processing everything. It's been a lot to take in."

Samantha didn't press further but watched Emily for a moment longer before returning to Alex.

Samantha: "There's another issue we need to address the mole within the agency. I have my suspicions, but I need you three to stay vigilant. Trust is our most valuable asset right now, and we can't afford to lose it."

Emily's face tightened slightly, but Alex didn't notice, too focused on the gravity of Samantha's words.

Alex: "We'll find the mole, Samantha. I won't let them tear this team apart."

Samantha: "I trust you, Alex. But be careful. This mission has already cost us too much. I don't want to lose any more of you."

The screen went dark as Samantha ended the call, leaving the room in a thick silence. Max busied himself, shutting down the laptop while Alex turned to the window, lost in his thoughts. Emily lingered near the door, her mind racing with conflicting emotions.

The next day started like any other, but the minute behavioral changes were hard to see. Emily went purposefully throughout the hotel room, her motions exact but with an underlying tension. She avoided Max's stare, her feet quick and deliberate, as though she was attempting to flee something just she could see. She would peek at Alex now and then when she felt no one else was watching, her eyes showing a combination of worry and something deeper, something she kept undercover.

Always the spectator, Max found it impossible to overlook the changes. He saw her distance and how her typically calm hands shook ever so little when she felt no one was observing. She appeared to be in another universe, her head somewhere totally. Max's attempts to start a discussion with her got courteous but detached answers. Every time he walked up to her, she would find a reason to distance herself a call she maintained she had to make, a paper she claimed required her right now, a sudden urge to check her phone. Her avoidance of him caused his suspicions to chew at him like an unrelenting itching he could not quite grasp.

Max chose to push a bit more at one point. He caught up with Emily as she stood at the window gazing at the city below.

Max: "Emily, are you okay? "

Emily: "I am good, Max." Simply a lot on my mind.

Max doubted it. He bent gently.

Max: "You can tell me whether something is off. We are in this together.

Emily's eyes flicked with something a spark of shame, maybe but it vanished as fast as it first showed. She forced a grin on him and rested a hand on his arm.

Emily: "Thanks for that, Max. But actually, I'm good.

She turned away before he could say anything further, leaving Max with growing discomfort. He watched her traverse the room, her posture rigid and her attention split. She attempted to disguise it, but the more she tried, the more confident he was that something was awry.

Alex, meantime, was engaged in the task. He painstakingly mapped possible sites where Volkov may attack next, hours at the table surrounded by maps and paperwork. His concentration was unflinching, his will unyielding. Every phone conversation, every piece of intelligence, every fresh information was another piece of the jigsaw he yearned to complete. His attention was fixed on the current work; the suspense in the room hardly registered with him. Still, the minute changes in the team were not invisible, even in his great concentration.

Alex looked up once, then saw Emily get some documents from the desk. Her motions were hesitant, and there was a disoriented air not there before. His gaze briefly turned to her, a flutter of fear crossing his face. Then, as if rejecting the idea, he returned to work, discounting any uncertainty that may divert him.

The day had a lot of activity stored for everyone as each was lost in their tasks. Alex stayed bent over the table, drawing locations on the map with a consistent beat with his pen. Max hung close by, his eyes darting to Emily, who was now sitting by the window, her eyes far off as she idly scrolled over her phone. Though each of them felt the widening gulf but was reluctant to express it, the once-solid team started fracturing at the margins. Max once drew Alex's eye and gently nodded towards Emily. Alex followed his eye and saw Emily appeared lost in contemplation, her often keen intellect appearing far away.

Max: "She's not yourself today."

Alex wrinkled his brow but shook his head.

Alex: "We all live under a great deal of strain. Her only processing is that."

Max wasn't sure, so he stopped further. Rather, he went back to his job; his mistrust grew with every instant. Although Alex was focused on the task, he couldn't eliminate the impression that something was changing inside their team a change that could not be disregarded any more.

***

The three of them assembled in the hotel room later that day. Max could not keep back anymore; he had been watching Emily with mounting anxiety all day. His discomfort had been chewing at him, and the idea of something going wrong among their close-knit crew was intolerable.

Max: "Emily, today you have been different. What's happening here?

Emily stammered at his directness, her composure temporarily breaking. Her eyes sparked with something fear, shame, or maybe both but she rapidly covered it with a false grin that missed her eyes.

Emily: "It's nothing, Max. Just the pressure. Everybody has gone through a great deal.

Max partially closed his eyes and looked at her face for responses she was not providing. Through her façade, he could see her hands shaking slightly as she held them together, and her voice wavers just enough to expose her.

Max: "Stress does not help you to avoid your team. Tell us if something seems off.

Emily's grin wavered as Max's comments sank on her. She opened her lips to reply, to say anything meant to allay his misgivings, but the words would not come. She was concealing something that worried her, but she couldn't let it out, not now, not when everything was precariously hanging.

Alex entered before Emily could muster the will to speak; his voice was calm but with a sharp edge of finality.

Alex: "Max, let it run off." Emily's right: every one of us is under great strain. Let us center on the goal. Max hesitated, looking at Alex and Emily alternately. Alex's eyes showed his trust, and it

was so pure that it left no space for doubt. But the same confidence made Max's stomach turn uncomfortably. Alex wanted to keep going and demand the truth, but his belief in Emily was unwavering. Max turned back reluctantly, swallowing his worry.

Max: "Fine. If anything is wrong, though, we must take action.

Emily sent Alex a thanks, her heart thumping in her chest. But that glance, that quiet conversation, carried something darker guilt. It tore at her, a constant pain that would not let her relax. She was hiding something, something she found difficult to bring herself to expose. Not just now. Not while the mission was online, and most definitely not when Alex's confidence in her was unflinching. For Alex, as well as for the task, she had to hold it together.

The team's fatigue became increasingly clear as the day dragged on. Emily's behavior kept shifting; her motions were more deliberate, and her acts more cautious. She seemed to be on edge, poised for something to break. She avoided Max's penetrating stare, and each time Alex spoke to her, she hesitated slightly a flutter of something she was trying so hard to suppress. Max had it in his bones, a mounting knowledge that something was wrong. The sense

that Emily was hiding something from them that may destroy the brittle equilibrium they were clinging to persisted with him.

Sitting at his laptop, apparently concentrated on his work, his eyes would dart to follow Emily when she was not looking. Every time he did, the anxiety in his chest tightened, and his ideas drifted from the task towards the divide that was gradually but developing in their team.

On the other hand, Emily sat at the brink of the bed much of the time, tapping frantically on her knee. Her head was a million miles away, her ideas entwined in a web of secrets she was not ready to reveal. Every sound made her jump; every look from Max or Alex seemed like a probe into her core. She was walking a tightrope and unsure of how long she may maintain her equilibrium.

Alex walked the room with his phone glued to his ear, blind to the conflict seething under the surface. He coordinated closely with their connections, with every call being a lifeline in the search for Volkov. Every piece of intelligence. His mind was a fortitude set on the current task, yet even in his concentration, a persistent sense that something wasn't right pulled at the margins of his awareness.

Driven by their anxieties and goals, they worked into the evening. The once-solid basis of trust that had kept them together was starting to weaken; the gaps widening with every hour were evidence. None of them could find themselves to express it; the weight of their whispered uncertainties was like an unseen, enormous force weighing down on them.

Alex was alone himself; the events of the preceding few days played in his head like a hurricane he could not flee. His mind kept Natalia's insults, the picture of the tattoo plaguing him, and the memory of his sister seemed like a wound never healing. But now, something fresh and disturbing nagged at the rear of his mind, something he couldn't really place.

A gentle knock on the door tore through his ideas. He turned to find Emily standing there, her face masked in worry.

Emily: "Alex, are you okay?"

Though it fell short of his eyes, Alex faked a grin. Indeed, simply thinking about it.

She entered and stared at him, her face softening. Her eyes revealed a warmth, a quiet assurance that they would negotiate this as always.

Emily: "Alex, we will make it through as always."

Alex nodded, her comments laying over him like a blanket. "I know Emily. It's good you're here.

Emily grinned back, but behind it, she felt darkness, something that dimmed her eyes and caused heart pain.

Emily: "Me too."

Alex sensed a flutter of hesitation as she exited the room a little doubt that poked at the rear of his consciousness. But he turned it aside right away.

He was not now able to afford diversions. The search for the mole had to go on even as the team's togetherness started to dissolve, the ties connecting them weaker with every secret, every whispered truth. The goal was too essential.

Chapter Seven: Counterintelligence

Natalia had always been a master of lies, a ghost able to pass through even the tightest of nets undetectable. Her reputation for always being one step ahead was the stuff of legends. For Alex and Max, this meant never being able to relax, always being on high alert, and knowing that every misstep may be their final. The strain was unrelenting, and the stakes were higher than ever because Natalia's counterintelligence strategies had them on edge.

Their game had evolved into a chess match, each action deliberate and each counter thoughtfully examined. Natalia, a ghost spinning a web of falsehoods and traps meant to confound, mislead, and disorient, had the upper hand, though. Her false leads moved and changed, always just out of grasp like shadows. Alex and Max had little option but to follow, but the ground under them seemed less secure with every stride.

One evening, Natalia laid her most recent trap. She carefully constructed and painstakingly detailed a false message she sent in one of their encrypted channels. The letter was straightforward enough a scheduled conference at an abandoned warehouse on the outskirts of the city but it was full of enough details to give it credibility. All of the time, the location and the putative participants all felt real, almost too true.

Alex and Max felt uneasy as they went over the message in their poorly lit safehouse. Reflecting their mental instability, the wavering light from one bulb creates extended shadows across the room.

Alex: "It might be a trap. It almost seems too perfect."

Usually, the pragmatic Max scowled as he studied the message, his eyes narrowing in focus. Every choice he made seemed weighty, and he might always be in danger right beyond the boundaries.

Max: "It may be, but what if it's real? This is not something we can afford to ignore."

Alex nodded, his mind caught between caution and the impulse to go. Though the nagging sensation that they were being played persisted, the specifics were too convincing to overlook.

Alex: "We need to be ready for anything."

For the next few hours, they meticulously went over every conceivable possibility. Alex examined and corrected their equipment, his hands moving with mechanical accuracy. His grip on his rifle revealed the stress; his eyes kept darting to the shadows as if anticipating something to come out of. Max quickly moved his fingers over the keyboard to create backup communication links, therefore guaranteeing they had an escape route should things go south. Though they were ready, there was a chill in the pit of their stomachs, neither of which they could shake. It was a chilly, creeping dread.

The night air was tense as they neared the warehouse; every breath they took felt weightier than the last. Before they stood the structure, its black, empty windows a quiet guardian in the evening, each step accentuated the sensation of approaching peril as the sound of gravel under their feet resonated in the quiet. Alex's senses sharpened, and every sound enhanced in the stifling quiet as his heart surged with their movement.

Their eyes searched the darkness for any movement, and they entered warily with guns drawn. As they descended farther into the large warehouse, their footsteps echoed back. The air was humid; their garments smelt of rust and rot. Every groan of the old building and rustling in the darkness alerted their senses. The message had been unambiguous, but the quiet they encountered was disturbing almost smothering.

Max: "This doesn't feel right."

Alex looked around; his instincts screamed to turn back. Something was awry, something they could feel in their bones but could not see.

Alex: "Keep on. We need to be certain."

They continued further into the building's guts, the strain between them a tight wire just about to break. The trap was sprung when they walked into the middle of the warehouse. Suddenly, all the lights of the warehouse turned on at once, blinding Alex and Max. Natalia's agents moved in from all sides at that moment. Alex and Max walked straight into an ambush, and the awareness struck them like a ton of bricks.

Alex: "It's a trap! We need to get out of here right now!"

Max was already moving, his weapon poised, and he aimed at the closest assailant. The sound of gunshots sharpened the air, echoing rounds bouncing off the metal walls. Every step, a battle, every breath, a struggle, they battled their way back towards the exit. Driven farther into the warehouse, Natalia's agents were unrelenting, their strikes exact and timed. The labyrinth of equipment and containers turned into a battleground, every turn perhaps fatal.

Still, Alex and Max were not unusual for close calls. Years of training started to flow, their motions a smooth ballet of survival as they negotiated the anarchy. Their gaze was strong, and they returned fire with lethal accuracy, hiding behind heaps of goods. Though the road was dangerous and full of rivals who knew the ground better than they did, the exit was in view.

Alex: "We nearly arrived! Maintain your mobility!"

They pressed on, bullets zipping by them as they dodged and negotiated the labyrinth of challenges. Though Natalia's agents weren't slowing down, the exit was just ahead. It was a limited getaway, the type that left your thoughts whirling and your heart thumping. They exploded through the doors, the frigid night air shocking them like a system collapse. The warehouse was filled with the noises of search behind them, but they continued. Breathing hard as adrenaline coursed through their veins, they sprinted till they arrived at the security of their automobile.

Alex looked at Max, his mouth tightened in annoyance as they rushed away from the warehouse. The events of the evening ran back into his head, each mistake and every moment of doubt.

Alex: "She had us where she wanted us the entire time!"

Equally annoyed, Max pounded his hand against the dashboard. His knuckles went white from his wrath.

Max: "Damn it! We should have seen that coming."

They both became tense, knowing they had been outmatched. Natalia had once more demonstrated her prowess, always in control. The close call had been too near, and the irritation ate at them, feeding their need to turn things around in their favor.

Alex and Max hurriedly gathered, determined not to be outmatched once more. They understood they had to turn against Natalia using her own strategies. Should she want to engage in dishonesty, they must also learn masters of that game. They had to feed her misleading information to produce a trail so strong she couldn't resist pulling the bait.

Alex: "We'll give her something to chew on if she wants to play mind games."

Max nodded, his thoughts rushing to design the ideal trap, which was already functioning technically.

Maxim: "Let's set the trap."

Over the following few hours, they painstakingly developed their scheme. Alex produced a fictitious data trail suggesting they had found crucial information about a new operation Natalia was allegedly preparing. The material was painstakingly crafted to be just genuine enough, full of the type of details Natalia could not resist. Knowing she watched their communications, they made sure the phony messages were put in areas she would come across.

Max worked on building a phony network for communication, complete with bogus alarms, and created plans. It was a careful balance making the material appear both safe enough and easily available to be worth Natalia's attention. They even recorded a message in Alex's voice telling their intended contacts to gather at a certain spot. The message was pressing, full of the type of urgency Natalia would have had to believe she was on something significant.

Max: "It needs to be compelling. We are done if she suspects anything."

Alex nodded, his thoughts already whirling forward to the next action. His voice clearly carried strain, but so did his determination.

Alex: "It will be. Now, we wait."

They did not have to wait long. Always alert, Natalia caught the communications as they were meant to be intercepted. Her agents sprung into action, headed directly for the bogus spot the instant she hooked the bait. From a distance, Alex and Max tracked every action, every mistake, as Natalia's crew fell into the trap.

It was clear how delighted one was to watch Natalia's agents running after shadows. They were the ones being outwitted, for once, and it provided Alex and Max the breathing space needed to compile important information. They followed the moves, charting Natalia's network's links and noting important players. If only momentarily, the tables had flipped, and it seemed like a small but important triumph.

Alex observed something unanticipated while tracking the procedure. Natalia herself arrived on the scene and guided her group with customary accuracy. Her cool head wavered, though, in a fleeting but clear instant.

She read a text message on her phone, and for a moment, her face softened to provide a glimmer of melancholy that felt inappropriate.

Alex fixed his gaze nowhere else. Natalia was not the merciless spy they had been fighting for so long in that little instant. She was human and vulnerable, and he related to her weakness in some way. Like a curtain being drawn back to see a side of her, he hadn't imagined. That moment stayed with him, a jigsaw piece that didn't quite fit but begged attention.

Max, concentrating on the goal, missed the change in Natalia. Alex, however, did. And he couldn't get it off his mind.

Later, when they went over the data they had gathered, Alex kept returning to that point. He couldn't help but wonder what had burst through Natalia's carefully put-on armor and what had caused her flutter of feeling. To say the least, it was disturbing and made him doubt all he knew about her.

Intrigued, Alex started researching Natalia's past in search of any hints to help explain what he had witnessed. He searched for anything that would help to clarify Natalia's true identity under the surface for hours, poring over papers and gathering previous reports. His findings startled him.

Natalia came from a background as complicated and agonizing as his own. Someone she had trusted deceived her profoundly, and that treachery had hurt someone she loved. Alex felt a sense of sorrow he hadn't expected as he went over the specifics of the story which was shockingly familiar. Natalia was driven by something more than simply power or allegiance to her cause despite her brutality. There was a wound there, one that hadn't healed, and that helped her to understand, if not justify her behavior.

Alex discovered his emotions for Natalia growing more complex as the bits of her past came together. Still, he considered her as an adversary, someone to be stopped. Now, though, he was unable to entirely separate anything else a mix of desire and empathy. Though it threatened to distort his judgment, it was a perilous sensation he could not ignore.

Alex: "She's more than just a target."

Raising an eyebrow, Max looked up from his work. He clearly displayed skepticism, but his anxiety was as evident.

Max: "What are you discussing?"

Alex hesitated as he knew that expressing his opinions would just make matters more difficult. He could sense the weight of his remarks and the possibility of altering the dynamics of their work.

Alex: "Nothing. Just -- just talking out loud."

Max did not press; he went back to work on current projects. But Alex's mind stayed on Natalia. He couldn't help but question her actual intentions and what motivated her to act as she did. Was it exactly retribution? A distorted view of justice? Alternatively, was it something very different?

Though he attempted to ignore such ideas, they persisted like a shadow at the brink of his consciousness. Still committed to uncovering the mole within the agency and thwarting Natalia's schemes, he remained concentrated on the goal. Now, though, he was unsure, a flutter of doubt that made him rethink all he knew.

He came to see from learning more about Natalia that their struggle transcended just power or control. It was personal for both of them, and that made it especially risky. Alex couldn't get rid of the impression that this was merely the beginning that the actual game had only just started that the stakes were bigger than ever before as the evening carried on.

Chapter Eight: High Stakes

Alex crouched low, the cold metal of the crates biting through his clothing. His pulse was steady, but his mind was anything but clear. With each structure shaped in the low light, he focused on the distant warehouse. The guards, the dark windows, and the aged metal cladding seemed so normal. But this was anything but routine. This was Volkov. This was everything.

Max shifted beside him, peering through his scope at the guards patrolling the entrance.

Max: "Five guards, two on the roof. It's going to be tight."

Alex nodded, signaling for silence as his mind flickered back to earlier that night.

***

Earlier: The Hotel Room

The hotel room smelled somewhat of cheap detergent and tobacco smoke. Though his thoughts kept drifting, Alex sat on the bed gazing at the warehouse map, every inch of it remembered by now. Max and Emily had been arguing about something about contingencies and exit routes, but Alex hadn't been listening.

Natalia's voice had been in his head all day. Her words from their last meeting still haunted him. Her cryptic warnings, how she had looked at him with those piercing eyes – he couldn't shake any of it. He tried to get that image out of his mind, but it was like a shadow that refused to leave. Emily's eyes flicked between Alex and Max, frustration simmering beneath her composed exterior. She had voiced her concerns several times, but Alex hadn't seemed to notice or care. His silence throughout the briefing was unnerving, and it wasn't the first time she had seen him this distracted. She glanced at him, her brow furrowed slightly. If they were going to make it out of this alive, Alex needed to be present. She had no room for error not when their lives were on the line. Max's voice had cut through the fog of his thoughts.

Max: "We go in through the south side, take out the perimeter guards first. Emily, you secured the arms shipment, and Alex and I will deal with Volkov."

Emily had nodded, her eyes darting to Alex, who still hadn't spoken.

Emily: "And what if something goes wrong? What's the fallback?"

Max had smirked, tapping the map.

Max: "We fight our way out. Simple."

Alex had stayed silent, but his stomach had twisted. He could feel the weight of the mission settling on his shoulders and, underneath it all, the weight of his thoughts about Natalia.

***

Present: The Warehouse

Unaware of the danger hiding in the shadows, the guards were approaching now. Alex shot back to the present as Max's hold on his firearm tightened. The cold bite of metal against his fingers brought him back to the present, but his mind couldn't shake the memories.

He blinked, the cold smell of the warehouse mixing with the cheap detergent of the hotel room. Natalia's voice whispered in the back of his mind, dragging him back to earlier that evening. He had to pay attention.

Moving in unison, they silently, quickly knocked down the first guard. Alex watched the other guards while Max hauled the body behind the containers. They slid through the door, their motions deliberate, exact.

Volkov was negotiating someplace within, and the dishonest official was with him. Alex's mind flickered again Natalia.

***

Earlier: A Meeting with Natalia

Alex had met Natalia at a remote café, distant from prying eyes, and it had been a wet evening with dense humidity. Her black coat gleamed with rain as she came late. Her eyes locked on his the instant she entered. Her face had been invisible.

Natalia: "You're playing a dangerous game, Alex."

He had bristled at her words but couldn't deny the truth in them.

Alex: "We're all playing games, Natalia. I'm just trying to win."

Natalia had been an enigma since the day they'd met, her loyalty always just out of reach. But this time, something had been different. The way her eyes lingered on him, the strange undertone in her voice it wasn't just a warning. It was something more. Something that kept Alex up at night, wondering if he was her pawn or her ally. Her cryptic smile had told him everything and nothing at once, as if she held the key to both his victory and his downfall.

She had leaned in closer, her voice lowering to a dangerous whisper.

Natalia: "You think you can win against Volkov? You don't even know the half of what he's capable of."

Her comments had troubled him, but it was how she had said them as though she knew more than she was revealing. Alex had attempted to ask her for information, but Natalia had just grinned coldly, a calculated smile that left more questions than answers.

***

Present: The Warehouse

As he and Max slipped farther into the warehouse, he carried the burden of that evening. His pulse thumped as he attempted to concentrate on the job. He studied the darkness, but Natalia's words kept returning to him. Max's quiet, eager voice broke through his thoughts.

Max: "We're almost at the center. Get ready."

They slipped around another stack of crates, moving toward the dim light that flickered ahead. And then they saw it Volkov, standing in the center of the room, flanked by heavily armed guards. The corrupt official stood beside him, gesturing toward the crates of weapons stacked neatly around them. The deal was happening right in front of them.

Max tightened his grip on his gun.

Max: "We take them now."

But something was wrong. Alex's instincts screamed at him to stop, to think. The situation felt like they were walking into a trap. He could feel his heart pounding in his ears, the moment's weight pressing down on him. And through it all, there was Natalia her face, her warnings. What was she playing at?

He hesitated, and that's when everything went to hell.

Gunfire erupted from the shadows, the mercenaries moving in from every side. Alex and Max dove behind a stack of crates as bullets pinged off the metal walls. Max shouted over the roar of the gunfire. Max: "It's an ambush!"

Alex fired blindly over the crates, his mind racing. They had walked right into it, and now they were pinned down, trapped. His thoughts scrambled, searching for a way out, but all he could think about was Natalia. *Was she behind this? Was she part of it?*

Emily's voice crackled through the earpiece, sharp with urgency.

Emily: "We're pinned on the other side! Alex, what's the plan?"

Alex's breath was coming in shallow gasps. This was his fault. He should have seen it coming and should have anticipated this. But he had been too distracted, too wrapped up in his own mind.

Alex: "Hold your position. We'll flank them."

Max glanced at him, his face grim.

Max: "You sure?"

Alex wasn't sure of anything anymore. But they had no other choice.

***

Earlier: The Hotel Room

Back in the cramped hotel room, Emily had been the first to voice her concerns.

Emily: "This isn't just another mission. Volkov's got people everywhere. We can't afford to mess this up."

Alex had stood near the window, his mind far off, but her words had brought him back. He had nodded, but the knot in his gut had just tightened. There was too much at stake too many moving parts. Max had been more optimistic.

Max: "We've dealt with worse."

But Alex had known, deep down, that this was different. And now, in the middle of the warehouse, with bullets flying around him, that feeling had only solidified.

***

Present: The Warehouse

They made their move, ducking and weaving through the hail of gunfire. Alex could feel the heat of the bullets as they whizzed past his head, but he kept moving, driven by a mixture of fear and desperation. They had to stop Volkov. They had to end this.

Max took out one of the guards with a well-placed shot. Max grunted, his leg buckling beneath him as the bullet grazed his thigh. Alex's heart pounded as he watched his friend falter, the sight of blood pooling beneath Max sending a jolt of panic through him. He couldn't afford to lose focus, not now. Not when they were so close.

Alex: "Max, you okay?" Max nodded, gritting his teeth against the pain.

Max: "Just a scratch."

Alex could see the strain in his eyes. Max was pushing through it, but they both knew it was bad. Alex tackled another to the ground, his fist connecting with the man's jaw before he could raise his weapon. But it wasn't enough. The guards kept coming, relentless in their assault.

And through it all, Alex couldn't stop thinking about Natalia. She was behind this, somehow. She had to be. The way she had warned him, the way she had looked at him this was her game, and he was caught in it.

Emily's voice came through the earpiece again, strained and desperate. Emily: "We're losing ground! Alex, we need backup!"

He could feel the tension between them like the edge of a knife and hear her voice screaming terror. She had noticed the gap between them and seen the way he had been sidetracked. Now, in the middle of the fight, it was all about to explode.

Max removed the rest of the guards with another round fired. Their breathing heavy and labored, they hurried fast to secure the arms cargo. Alex was on him in a minute, throwing him to the ground and cuffing his hands behind his back as the crooked official tried to leave.

But, the cost of the endeavor became obvious when they reorganized. Max was dragging, a gunshot grazing his leg. Now Emily's voice was quiet, her irritation evident on the earpiece. Alex dabbed at the perspiration on his brow, his head still whirling with Natalia.

They had stopped the deal. They had captured the key players. But at what cost?

As they made their way out of the warehouse, the adrenaline still pumping through their veins, Alex couldn't shake the feeling that this was only the beginning. The fallout from the mission would be brutal emotionally and physically. And Natalia… she was still out there, still pulling the strings.

Max clapped him on the back, his voice rough from the fight.

Max: "We got them. But it was too close."

Alex nodded, but he was thinking elsewhere. He could see the tension on the squad, and through it all, Natalia's face stayed in his memory like a storm building on the horizon. With her warnings and her terrible presence, He realized his grasp on him was beginning to pull everything apart. He could not avoid her.

As they walked out into the night, Emily fell into step beside him, her silence heavy, her face hard with anger and something darker. She didn't even have to say anything Alex could feel the tension radiating off her. He knew exactly what she was thinking, knew that she had seen through his distraction, felt it in the cracks between them.

Finally, she broke the silence, her voice tight with frustration.

Emily: "You weren't with us back there."

Alex blinked, surprised by her bluntness, but the accusation was impossible to deny.

Alex: "What are you talking about? We completed the mission."

Emily stopped walking, forcing him to stop, too. Her eyes were burning with barely restrained anger.

Emily: "You think I didn't notice? You were distracted, Alex. You've been distracted for weeks. This isn't just about the mission anymore; it's about you not being able to focus and not seeing what's right in front of you."

Alex's jaw clenched, a thousand retorts rising to his lips, but none of them came out. She wasn't wrong. He had been distracted, but what was he supposed to say? That Natalia was the reason? That every time he closed his eyes, he could see her, hear her voice?

Max, sensing the tension between them, lingered a few feet away, his gaze flicking nervously between them but saying nothing.

Emily took a step closer, her voice lowering, more personal now, more raw.

Emily: "It's her, isn't it? Natalia. She's in your head."

Alex's breath caught in his throat, his mind spinning. How had she known? How could she have seen what even he was barely able to admit to himself?

He didn't answer, but that only seemed to confirm her suspicions. Emily let out a short, bitter laugh, shaking her head in disbelief.

Emily: "I can't believe this. We almost died tonight, Alex. And you your mind was somewhere else. With her."

Alex's heart hammered in his chest.

Alex: "It's not like that."

Emily scoffed, her eyes narrowing.

Emily: "Then what is it like? Because from where I'm standing, it looks like you're more concerned about whatever the hell is going on with her than you are about this team. About us."

Her words stung, cutting deeper than Alex wanted to admit. And for a brief, painful moment, he saw the truth in her anger. He had been distracted. He had been letting Natalia get into his head, and it was affecting everything.

Emily turned away from him, her voice cold, final.

Emily: "You need to figure out where your loyalties lie, Alex. Because right now, it sure as hell doesn't feel like it's with us."

She walked away, leaving him standing there, alone, in the dark. Max gave him a look part sympathy, part concern but didn't say anything. He didn't need to. Alex could feel the strain between them, could feel the weight of Emily's words hanging in the air, suffocating him.

***

Earlier: A Meeting with Natalia

It had been one of those quiet, tense moments. Natalia had leaned in closer to him, her dark eyes holding his.

Natalia: "You can't trust anyone, Alex. Not even yourself."

Her words stuck with him like an itch he was unable to get at. She had always understood how to enter his skull, how to gently skew his ideas to cause him to doubt everything. And now, all Alex could think about was whether she had been right after a mission that ought to have felt like a triumph.

***

Present: The Warehouse

The warehouse was still behind them, the sounds of the firefight echoing in the distance. Alex stumbled forward, his shoulder throbbing, the pain spreading through his body like fire. They hadn't escaped yet, but they were close. Too close. The mission wasn't complete not even close but survival was the priority right now.

Max's voice rang in his ear, frantic and hoarse. Max: "We need to get to the truck now!"

But Alex could barely process the words. His mind was spinning, the weight of everything crashing down on him the mission, the ambush, the looming presence of Natalia. She had saved them, but *why? Why now? Why had she stepped in just when they were on the brink of collapse?*

Emily was still ahead, her figure barely visible through the haze of smoke. She was moving toward the exit, toward safety. But something was wrong. Alex could feel it in the pit of his stomach. The battle wasn't over. Not yet.

As they approached the truck, Alex's vision blurred for a moment, his pulse racing. They had captured the weapons. They had stopped the arms deal, but something was missing. Something critical. His instincts screamed that they weren't safe, that this mission had more layers than he could see. And the line between ally and enemy had never been so unclear.

Suddenly, the sharp sound of boots on the gravel made Alex freeze. He turned just in time to see a figure step out from behind a row of crates. It was Emily.

But she wasn't alone.

Volkov was beside her, his hand resting lightly on her shoulder, a grin spreading across his face. The world seemed to slow as Alex's breath caught in his throat.

Emily looked back at him, her face unreadable, but there was something in her eyes something cold, something final. The reality of her betrayal hit him like a punch to the gut.

Alex's mind drifted again to Natalia the night they met had been just as tense, her words as cryptic. She had warned him about the danger, but it was always layered like she knew something he didn't. The way she looked at him across the dimly lit café table, her eyes a shade darker than the room, had stuck with him. Now, with Emily gone, her words came crashing back with a chilling clarity. Natalia had always played a game deeper than he could see.

Volkov's voice was like ice.

Volkov: "Well, Alex, it seems we've all been playing our own games."

Before Alex could even react, everything erupted into chaos once more.

Chapter Nine: Betrayal

Alex's breath came in quick, ragged rushes as the truth of Emily's treachery sank over him like a weight too great to carry. The shock was real; it grabbed his chest and made breathing difficult. He gazed at her, his mind faltering to fit the icy figure now standing next to Viktor Volkov against the lady he had trusted for so long.

Everything around him the fight, the sound of gunfire, Max yelling vanished from view. Just Emily was visible to him. Her gaze fixed on his with a force that twisted his gut. Her glance revealed no regret. Not at all hesitant. Just cold, steely resolve. Volkov's hand rested casually on her shoulder, a twisted smile playing on his lips.

Volkov: "You never saw it coming, did you, Alex?"

Alex barely heard him. His mind raced as he tried to piece together the events of the past few weeks. The warning signs had been there Emily's growing distance, her impatience, the silent resentment simmering between them but he had been too distracted by Natalia.

Natalia. She had been a storm, disrupting everything. Her arrival had shifted the entire dynamic of the team. She wasn't just a key asset in the mission - she was the mission. Alex had devoted every moment to understanding her, unlocking her secrets. Natalia's ability to gather intelligence had become their primary focus, and everything revolved around her. But had it blinded him to everything else? Had his obsession with her role in bringing down Volkov been the catalyst for Emily's betrayal?

Emily: "You were so focused on her... on Natalia. You weren't paying attention to what was happening right in front of you."

Her words were like a knife twisting in his chest. She wasn't wrong. He had allowed Natalia's presence to overshadow everything. Even now, with her involvement in the mission still uncertain, he couldn't deny the magnetic pull she had exerted on him. Was it because of her unparalleled skills? Or something more?

Alex: "Emily… how long?"

His voice was scratchy, little more than a whisper. He wasn't sure he wanted to hear the answer. Emily's face didn't soften, but there was a flicker of something in her eyes perhaps regret or a fleeting moment of guilt.

Emily: "Long enough."

Alex's stomach churned as bile rose in his throat. He wanted to speak, to shout, to make sense of it all, but the words caught in his throat. His hands tightened around his weapon; it was the only thing keeping him from falling apart. Max's voice broke through the haze.

Max: "Emily, you don't have to do this. We can fix this."

For a brief second, Emily's eyes flickered to Max. Alex could see the woman they had fought alongside, the one who had been with them through every mission, every battle. But it was gone as quickly as it appeared, replaced by the cold, impenetrable mask she now wore.

Emily: "It's too late, Max. It's already done."

Max froze his horror at Emily's comments like a sledgehammer striking him. He had looked on her as a sister in arms and trusted her. Though his head spun, attempting to make sense of it, the fact was indisputable. Emily had started looking toward them. His fingers tightened into fists, and the injury in his leg lost importance as fury surged inside him.

Max: "Why, Emily? Why did you do this?"

But she didn't even look at him. Her gaze was locked on Alex, cold and unforgiving. Volkov, ever the opportunist, chuckled softly.

Volkov: "She made her choice, Alex. And I must say, she's been quite valuable."

Volkov took a step forward, his grin widening.

Volkov: "You see, Alex, loyalty is such a fragile thing, isn't it? It is so easy to break, so easy to bend to your will. You've been so focused on winning your little war with me that you forgot to look behind you. Isn't that what makes this so delicious? Your biggest weakness wasn't your enemy it was your trust in your team. And now, look where that's left you."

Alex's grip on his weapon tightened, anger flaring hot in his chest. He forced himself to focus, forced himself to think. They were in the middle of an operation. Volkov was still a threat, and they needed to stop him. But every instinct screamed at Alex to get answers, to understand how things had gotten to this point.

The words hit Alex like a freight train, each syllable embedding itself in his chest. Emily's betrayal had cracked something inside him, something fundamental.

How had he let this happen? How had he missed the signs? He replayed every conversation, every glance, every small moment of doubt he'd pushed aside over the past weeks. It was all so clear now. The arguments, the distance, the way she'd stopped meeting his eyes when they talked about the mission. How could he have been so blind? Was it because of Natalia? His gut twisted at the thought how much of this was his fault? His obsession with Natalia, the shadow she cast over his every move, kept him from seeing the truth right before him.

Alex: "Why, Emily? Why did you do this?"

Her voice was softer this time, barely above a whisper.

Emily: "You stopped being there for us, Alex. You stopped being there for me."

Her words echoed in his mind. How many times had he brushed off her concerns, been too absorbed in his obsession with Natalia to see what was happening right in front of him? Emily's expression was cold, but underneath it, Alex could sense the weight of her words.

Emily: "You weren't there, Alex. Every mission, every step, you were a million miles away. And it wasn't just about Natalia. It was everything. You stopped seeing me. Stopped seeing what this team needed. You were so caught up in your own war that you forgot we were fighting it. I couldn't wait around for you to figure it out anymore. Volkov offered me a way out a chance to survive, to do more than just be a pawn in your game. You left me no choice, Alex. This was survival."

The guilt settled deep in Alex's chest. He had always prided himself on being the leader, the one who held the team together. But now, in the aftermath of Emily's betrayal, he saw how far he had fallen. He hadn't been the leader Emily needed. His obsession with Natalia and his constant focus on the mission had driven a wedge between them, one that couldn't be repaired.

Volkov: "It's time to go, Emily."

Emily nodded, but her eyes lingered on Alex for just a moment longer, something unreadable flickering behind them. Then she turned, walking away with Volkov, leaving Alex and Max standing there, shell-shocked and broken.

The silence left in Emily's wake was deafening. Max stumbled forward, his injured leg slowing him down, but the weight of what had just happened was heavier than any physical wound. Alex's mind raced. They had lost Emily not just physically, but mentally. How had it come to this? How had he missed the signs? Alex's grip tightened around his gun as he stared after her. He couldn't focus, not on the mission, not on their escape. All he could think about was the look in her eyes. The team was shattered, and it was his fault. Max's voice was thick with anger, his fists clenched.

Max: "We need to move. Now!"

Alex nodded numbly, the weight of everything crashing down on him all at once. The mission wasn't over. Volkov was still out there. But the betrayal was too raw, too fresh. It left a hole in his chest, one that he didn't know how to fill.

As they exited the warehouse, Alex's mind was a blur of conflicting emotions. He had trusted Emily. He had counted on her. And now, she was gone, standing with their enemy.

The lines between ally and enemy had blurred, and Alex wasn't sure he could trust anyone anymore not even himself.

Later, outside the Warehouse, The night air hit him like a shock, cold and unforgiving. Alex stumbled slightly as they moved toward the truck, the pain in his shoulder flaring with each step. The mission was falling apart around them, and all he could think about was the look in Emily's eyes the hardness, the resolve. Max climbed into the driver's seat, his face grim, his jaw clenched.

Max: "We'll figure this out, Alex. We'll stop them."

But Alex wasn't so sure. Everything felt like it was slipping through his fingers, and he wasn't sure how to pull it back. The betrayal cut deep, but so did the doubts plaguing him for weeks. Doubts about Natalia. Doubts about his judgment.

The walls closing in and the planet whirling out of control made him feel. Emily's treachery was the last nail in the coffin everything he had created, every link he believed he could rely on, broken instantly. His remaining was what? A shattered squad, a damaged sense of trust, and a conflict he knew he could not win anymore. He turned to Max, the hurt in his friend's eyes, the unsaid charge Alex had let them all down. He was unable to ignore it. For weeks now, they had all been disintegrating; he had been too preoccupied with Volkov and Natalia to realize it. Alex felt more alone than ever as the weight of the treachery fell over him.

Alex sat back against the seat as the vehicle roared to life; his thoughts spun with the weight of everything. Though the goal was far from done, much had already been lost. And far away, darker and more deadly than ever, the shadows of treachery and dishonesty persisted.

Chapter Ten: The False Lead

Alex stood still, his eyes locked on the door Emily had walked out of during their last mission. The room felt empty, suffocating even, as the betrayal hung heavy between him and Max, like a third presence neither could shake. His fingers traced the lines on the map before him, but his mind wasn't on the route. His thoughts drifted, replaying the scene over and over the coldness in Emily's eyes, the way she had turned her back on them without hesitation. He could still hear the sound of her footsteps fading. With each step, another nail hammered into the coffin of their trust. Alex's chest tightened, his breath shallow as guilt clawed at his insides. His focus slipped, just like everything else lately.

Max's voice cut through his thoughts, sharp and abrupt.

Max: "Alex, focus."

Max wasn't looking at him. His eyes were fixed on the maps and scattered documents strewn across the table. His leg throbbed from the wound he had taken during the last ambush, but his silence was worse than his pain an unspoken indictment. Alex didn't need to hear the words to feel Max's disappointment; it clung to the air between them, heavy and sour like a bitter aftertaste.

Alex: "I'm trying, Max. But every plan feels wrong now. Every move we make... it's like she's always one step ahead."

The weakness in his own voice grated on him, but he couldn't help it. The wound Emily had left was still fresh, and it festered in every decision, every strategy he tried to form. Max shifted slightly, his hand instinctively brushing his injured leg. His jaw clenched as he spoke, his voice low and steady a calm in the storm, though even that calm felt brittle now.

Max: "Then stop thinking about her. She's not our concern anymore. Volkov is. Do you want to take him down or not? If yes, then forget about Emily."

Alex bit back the retort that burned in his throat. Easier said than done, he thought bitterly. Emily had been more than a teammate; she'd been a constant, someone he could trust. Now she was gone, and the void left in her wake threatened to swallow everything. His hand tightened over the edge of the map, knuckles white, as if holding onto the paper might stop the rest of the world from slipping out of his grasp.

He looked down at the map, eyes scanning the routes, but the lines blurred. The docks. It had to be the docks. They could lure Volkov there, use false intel, and set the trap. But his gut twisted with the gnawing thought: What if Emily had already sold them out? What if this was yet another trap, another layer of deception?

Alex: "We make Volkov think we're hitting the warehouse at the docks. He'll send his men, and we'll trap him."

Max didn't respond immediately. His face remained impassive, but Alex caught the flicker of doubt in his eyes, a tiny crack in the mask. Max leaned forward, resting his elbows on the table.

Max: "What if she's already compromised that? What if she's setting us up again?"

Alex's fists clenched, nails digging into his palms. Frustration bubbled up, hot and sharp. Max was voicing the very thoughts Alex had been fighting against. The problem was Max was right.

Alex: "We don't have a choice, Max. If we wait any longer, we lose everything. It's now or never."

Max leaned back in his chair, exhaling slowly. His hands gripped the armrests tightly as if bracing himself for another blow.

Max: "Fine. But if this is another trap, we're done."

They both knew what that meant. If this went wrong, there wouldn't be a second chance.

***

The docks were shrouded in fog, the faint sounds of water lapping against the ships echoing in the distance. Towering cranes stood like skeletal giants against the night sky, rusted arms reaching out as if to grab the unwary. Every container loomed over Alex and Max, casting jagged, shifting shadows across their path as they edged closer to the warehouse. The air was thick with the smell of salt and metal, the distant creaking of ships adding to the unease.

Alex's grip tightened on his weapon, every nerve on edge. The ground beneath his boots felt unstable, as though he was walking on glass that could shatter at any moment. Max limped slightly behind, his injury slowing him, but his gun was raised and ready.

They moved in silence, their breaths shallow and deliberate. Each step forward felt like they were sinking deeper into a trap they couldn't see. The weight of unspoken doubts pressed down on Alex, but there was no turning back now. His mind flickered to Emily, her cold expression, and how she had looked at him like a stranger. He shook the thought away, forcing his focus back on the task.

Max's voice broke the silence, a low growl barely louder than a whisper.

Max: "This doesn't feel right."

Alex didn't respond. He could feel the unease that settled in his gut, thick and heavy, like the fog surrounding them. But there was no room for hesitation. The warehouse loomed ahead, its shadow stretching like a dark omen over the water.

Then, the first shot rang out.

Max: "It's a trap!"

They dropped to the ground, rolling behind a stack of crates as bullets ricocheted off the steel containers surrounding them. The noise was deafening, a sudden burst of chaos that shattered the silence of the docks. Alex pressed his back against a container, his heart hammering in his chest. The sharp, acrid scent of gunpowder filled the air, mixing with the salty sea breeze that now felt more like a stinging slap than a refreshing gust.

Alex: "Move!"

Max winced as he shifted, his leg slowing him down, but he pushed forward, gritting his teeth against the pain. They darted between cover, Alex returning fire whenever he caught a glimpse of their attackers shadows darting between containers, too fast and too well-hidden to get a clear shot.

Another explosion rocked the ground to their left, sending debris crashing around them. The force knocked Alex off balance, and he hit the ground hard, feeling the impact vibrate through his entire body. His vision blurred momentarily, the world spinning as dust and smoke filled the air, choking his lungs. Max's voice cut through the haze, snapping him back to the moment.

Max: "We're pinned down! We need to move!"

Alex fired blindly into the shadows, trying to suppress the attackers, but his mind kept circling back to the same thought: Emily knew. She tipped them off. This was her doing. He hesitated, and that moment of distraction nearly cost them both. A mercenary charged from the side, his gun aimed directly at Max. Alex saw him just in time, instinct taking over as he pulled the trigger. The mercenary fell, his body crumpling to the ground before he could fire.

Alex: "We're getting out of here."

Max nodded, pushing forward, limping through the maze of crates and debris. Explosions continued to rock the ground beneath them, the air thick with dust and smoke. Each breath tasted of ash, burning the back of Alex's throat. They ducked and wove through the chaos, but it felt like the world was closing in on them, the noose tightening with every step.

Finally, they broke through the line of fire, reaching the edge of the docks. Both of them were bruised, their breaths coming in ragged gasps, their bodies aching from the relentless assault. But they were alive for now.

***

Back at the safe house, the walls seemed to close in on Alex, shrinking with every failed mission, every wrong move. He paced the room like a caged animal, his hands clenched into fists, his breaths coming in short, ragged bursts. The mission had failed. Again. And all because he couldn't keep his head straight. The weight of it was crushing, pressing down on him like the ceiling might collapse.

Max sat with his leg propped up, his face a mask of pain and frustration. His silence was louder than any words he could have spoken. When he finally spoke, his voice was calm, but the disappointment was unmistakable, like a slow, deliberate knife wound.

Max: "We can't keep doing this, Alex."

Alex stopped mid-step, turning to face him. His chest heaved with the effort of holding back the tide of guilt, frustration, and anger that threatened to spill over.

Alex: "What do you want me to say, Max? I know I screwed up. I know this is my fault."

Max shifted in his seat, his expression unreadable. His leg throbbed, but he barely flinched. His eyes, however, spoke volumes, a cold distance settling in them.

Max: "I expect you to lead. That's it. Stop getting us into these traps. You've been too distracted for too long, and it's killing us."

The words hit harder than any bullet. Alex flinched, but deep down, he knew Max was right. Every mission, every plan, had been tainted by his obsession with Emily and Natalia. He had let them cloud his judgment, and now they were paying the price. The hole Emily had left behind grew wider by the minute, threatening to swallow everything they'd worked for.

Alex: "I'll fix it, Max. No more mistakes."

Max didn't respond, but the silence that followed was deafening. The trust between them was hanging by a thread, and Alex could feel it fraying, unraveling with every second.

***

Hours passed, and Alex stood by the window, staring into the darkened sky. His mind churned with thoughts of betrayal, failure, and Volkov's next move. But amidst the chaos in his head, something began to clear, like a fog lifting. It wasn't just about Emily anymore. It wasn't just about her walking away.

Emily's betrayal hadn't been as simple as it seemed. She hadn't just walked away to save herself. She had led them to Volkov's weakest point. It was subtle, buried under layers of deception, but it was there clearer now in hindsight. The docks had been a distraction, a false lead. The real target was elsewhere. And now, with a new clarity, Alex could see it.

Emily hadn't betrayed them out of malice she had been trying to point them in the right direction, even as she walked away. He turned to Max, who was resting but still alert, his eyes following Alex's every move with quiet intensity.

Alex: "I've been thinking… Emily wasn't just leading us into traps. There's something else. We've been focused on the wrong thing. We need to change our approach."

Max raised an eyebrow, skepticism flickering in his eyes, but he listened.

Max: "What are you saying?"

Alex's eyes narrowed, his voice steady for the first time in what felt like weeks.

Alex: "Volkov's been playing us, but there's a pattern. I think I know where to hit him next. This time, we won't miss."

Max met his gaze, the tension still thick between them, but something shifted. There was an understanding now. They were battered and broken but not defeated. Not yet.

Alex: "We're going to take Volkov down, Max. No distractions. This time, we finish it."

For the first time in weeks, the path ahead was beginning to clear. They had one more shot, and they wouldn't miss this time.

Chapter Eleven: Fractured Trust

Alex sat at the small, worn table, papers scattered before him. His eyes traced the lines on the maps, but his mind was elsewhere on Emily, on Natalia, and on Volkov. The plan to stop Volkov's attack on New York hung over him like a dark cloud, looming with the weight of imminent disaster. Every decision felt fraught with danger. Every step seemed to lead them deeper into uncertainty, into chaos.

Across from him, Max sat with his leg stretched out and bandaged, the pain evident in his grim expression. The silence between them was sharper than words. Max didn't need to speak his gaze, the way his eyes never quite met Alex's, said everything. The room felt heavier with each unspoken accusation, with the trust that frayed further with every passing second.

Alex: "We need to move forward."

Max's gaze flicked up, his jaw tightening. His frustration was clear in the way his fists clenched, in the rigid set of his shoulders. But he didn't respond immediately. Instead, he leaned back in his chair, his hands resting on his knees as though physically holding back his anger.

Max: "Forward? Where, exactly, Alex? Every plan we've made so far has fallen apart. We're barely keeping our heads above water, and you still think we can just 'move forward'?"

Alex clenched his jaw, the tension in his own body mirroring Max's. Max's words stung, not because they weren't true, but because they echoed his own thoughts. Every plan had crumbled Emily's betrayal, the ambush at the docks, and now the constant weight of Natalia's presence. It was all unraveling. Alex could feel the thread slipping through his fingers, too thin to hold onto.

Alex: "We don't have a choice. Volkov is planning something big, and if we don't act soon, we'll be too late. New York is the target. We can't sit here and do nothing."

Max's expression hardened, his eyes narrowing as his hands curled into fists on the table.

Max: "And what about her?"

The venom in Max's voice was unmistakable. He didn't need to name her Alex knew exactly who he was talking about. Natalia. Her presence had become a wedge between them, a growing point of contention with every passing day. Max had never trusted her, and after Emily's betrayal, that distrust had only deepened and solidified like concrete between them.

Before Alex could respond, the door creaked open. Natalia stepped inside, her movements quiet and deliberate. Her eyes flicked between them, sensing the tension hanging thick in the air. There was no smile, no calculated expression just exhaustion and something else... a vulnerability Alex hadn't seen before.

Natalia: "I have information."

Her voice broke the silence, but it didn't ease the tension. If anything, it made the air between them heavier, as though it was pressing down on all of them. Alex could feel Max's eyes boring into him, silently asking the question Alex didn't want to answer: Can we trust her?

Alex turned to face Natalia, his voice cold and guarded.

Alex: "What kind of information?"

Natalia stepped further into the room, her movements deliberate but weary. She had always been poised, in control, but now there was something raw in her posture, something unguarded. She crossed her arms, a defensive gesture, but Alex caught the slight tremble in her fingers a tremble she quickly stilled.

Natalia: "Volkov is accelerating his plans. He's moving sooner than we thought. If you want to stop him from attacking New York, you'll need me. But I can't do this alone I need protection. Volkov wants me dead as much as he wants to destroy you."

Max let out a sharp, bitter laugh, shaking his head as he pushed himself to his feet, his leg trembling from the effort.

Max: "Convenient. You're always at risk, aren't you? Always needing something from us."

Natalia's eyes flicked toward Max, but she didn't flinch. She had grown used to his hostility, his suspicion. She stood her ground, her voice steady but quieter.

Natalia: "Believe what you want, but without me, you don't stand a chance. Volkov knows your moves and your tactics. I'm the only one who knows how he operates his weaknesses."

Max took a step forward, his voice low, a growl simmering beneath the surface.

Max: "And how do we know you're not just feeding us more lies? Like Emily did?"

The room felt charged, like a fuse waiting to ignite. Alex stood up slowly, his gaze shifting between Max and Natalia, the tension palpable, thickening with every second. His voice, when he finally spoke, was calm but undercut with a steel edge.

Alex: "That's enough."

Max shot him a look, his frustration bubbling beneath the surface, unspoken but loud. Alex could feel the trust between them crumbling further, the weight of their shared history no longer enough to hold it together.

Max: "You really think we can trust her? After everything?"

Alex exhaled, running a hand over his face. He didn't know. He wasn't sure of anything anymore. But what choice did they have? Every move felt like a gamble, every decision a risk they couldn't afford to ignore.

Alex: "We don't have a choice, Max. We need her information. We need every advantage we can get."

Max's face was a mask of disbelief, but he didn't argue. Instead, he limped toward the window, staring out into the night, his silence heavy with unspoken resentment.

***

As the hours passed, Alex and Natalia found themselves working late into the night, poring over maps and intel. Max had retreated to rest, leaving the two of them alone in the small room. The silence between them wasn't hostile, but it was tense, heavy with everything that had happened and everything that remained unsaid.

Natalia leaned over the table, her finger tracing a series of coordinates.

Natalia: "Volkov's moving faster than we thought. If we hit this location, we might be able to cut off his supply chain. But it won't be easy."

Alex nodded, but his mind wasn't entirely on the logistics of the mission. His thoughts kept drifting, pulled between the operation and the growing bond between him and Natalia. It was strange despite everything, despite her past, despite the manipulations he knew she was capable of there was a connection between them. They were both broken, both carrying burdens too heavy for most to understand.

Natalia's voice pulled him back to the present.

Natalia: "Alex?"

He blinked, focusing on her face. She looked tired, worn down in a way he hadn't noticed before. There was a vulnerability in her eyes, something raw she had hidden behind her sharp exterior.

Alex: "I'm listening."

She studied him for a moment, her expression softening. There was no defiance in her gaze, no calculated manipulation just an exhausted truth.

Natalia: "You're not, but that's okay. I know you don't trust me. I wouldn't trust me either."

Alex let out a soft chuckle, surprising even himself with the sound.

Alex: "It's not about trust. It's about survival. We both have something to gain here."

Natalia leaned back, crossing her arms. Her posture was less guarded now, more resigned.

Natalia: "We're not so different, you and I. We've both had to make impossible choices. We've both lost people. Maybe we're both just trying to survive this mess."

Her words hung in the air, and for a moment, Alex didn't know how to respond. He hadn't expected this this openness from her. He hadn't expected to feel anything at all.

Alex: "Maybe."

***

By morning, Max rejoined them at the table. His face was pale, his leg clearly bothering him, but his focus remained sharp. The three of them went over the final details of the operation. Volkov's plans to attack New York were clearer now, thanks to Natalia's information. They had a narrow window to intercept him, but the risks were higher than ever.

Max leaned over the map, pointing to a specific route.

Max: "We hit the convoy first. If we can disrupt his supplies, it'll slow him down. But we need to be ready for an ambush."

Alex nodded, trying to focus on the mission, but the tension between Max and Natalia was still thick, hanging over them like a storm about to break.

Natalia: "Volkov will anticipate that move. He'll have a backup, so we need to be ready for anything."

Max shot her a look, but he didn't argue. He was still skeptical of her, still waiting for the moment she'd betray them, but for now, he kept his silence.

Chapter Twelve: The Final Showdown

Alex stared at the walls of the safe house. Like a thick veil, the weight of past events, including Emily's betrayal and the chaos of recent missions, descended upon him. Max sat opposite, his leg up and discomfort visible on his face. Though they had barely missed their last assignment, they had no time to heal. Time was running short, and Volkov's preparations exceeded their ability to keep up.

The buzz of Alex's phone broke the oppressive quiet. Max raised his guarded yet vigilant gaze. Alex grabbed the gadget, and his brows wrinkled as he read the message. One of their last surviving friends came from a trustworthy source. Max immediately saw the change in Alex's demeanor something deep had just dropped into their laps.

Alex: "It's worse than we thought. Volkov isn't just targeting the city's infrastructure. He's planning to hit the Global Summit in New York. All those world leaders in one place he's going to use it as a stage to destabilize everything."

They had known Volkov was planning something big, but this was beyond anything they had anticipated. A direct attack on international leaders would be catastrophic, triggering a chain reaction of global chaos.

Max: "When?"

Alex set the phone down.

Alex: "Two days. He's leveraging a multi-layered attack cyber, physical, everything. If we don't stop him, it's game over."

The reality of the situation hit like a punch to the gut. They couldn't afford any more mistakes. This was the turning point where everything had to change no more defense. No more reacting. It was time to take the fight to Volkov directly.

Alex: "We regroup right now. We hit him where it hurts."

The resolve in Alex's voice was unmistakable. He looked at Max, and for the first time in days, Max saw the fire that had once defined Alex the unyielding determination to see this through, no matter the cost. They had been on the back foot for too long, but this was their chance to turn the tide. Alex called the emergency meeting. Every face around the table bore the marks of exhaustion but also a fierce determination that the urgency of their mission had rekindled. Natalia sat on one end, her eyes locked on the map of New York displayed on the screen. Max was beside her, his leg still bandaged but his spirit unbroken. They were all battle-worn, but this was it the final push.

Alex: "Listen up. Volkov's targeting the Global Summit. We have 48 hours to stop him. This isn't just about us anymore but about preventing a global disaster. Here's the plan."

He tapped on the map, highlighting key locations: the summit venue, the city's major infrastructure points, and Volkov's suspected safe houses. Every spot was a potential target, and every minute counted.

Alex: "Max, you'll be our lead on cyber warfare. Your job is to get into Volkov's network, disrupt his communication channels, and gain control of the security systems at the summit. He can't execute his plan if he can't talk to his men."

Max: "I'll have it locked down. No one gets in or out without us knowing."

Alex turned to Natalia, whose expertise in counter-intelligence was unmatched. Despite their fractured trust, they needed her now more than ever.

Alex: "Natalia, you'll coordinate our intelligence operations. Monitor every feed, every movement. We need eyes on Volkov at all times. You've worked with him; you know how he thinks. I need you to anticipate his next move."

Natalia: "He's going to expect resistance. We need to stay ahead of him and be unpredictable. I'll track his communications and movements."

Alex: "I'll handle ground operations. Coordinate with NYPD and federal agents. We need to secure the summit venue and eliminate any threats on-site. This will be a fight, and we must be ready for anything."

Alex paused, letting the weight of their mission settle over them. This was more than just a tactical operation their chance to make things right, to strike back against the man who had been a constant shadow over their lives. He looked around the room, meeting each of their gazes.

Alex: "We've lost a lot. We've been betrayed. But this team is stronger than any one of us. We stop Volkov here. We stop him now."

Everyone scattered and headed to their stations, their responsibilities clear and their will restored. This was their last posture. Alex realized they were ready for whatever came next as he watched them go. The battle lines were established, and they were moving on the offensive this time.

***

The high-security location where the Global Summit was taking place was a fortification walls strengthened with cutting-edge protection, armed guards monitoring every access, and surveillance systems allowing no area to be neglected. From the outside, it appeared impenetrable, evidence of the force it shielded. For Alex and his group, however, it was only one more challenge on their road to intercept Viktor Volkov.

Alex bent low behind a parked van, his eyes fixed on the entryway where police in tactical gear moved with exacting accuracy. His earpiece faintly hummed with Max's voice, reporting on the security systems.

Max: "The main access point is locked down tight. They have thermal sensors, motion detectors, and at least three backup systems. It's going to be a nightmare getting through."

Alex surveyed the route ahead. Natalia was nearby, her fingers tapping rapidly on a portable console, working to turn off the digital barriers between them and Volkov. The team was spread out, each taking on their assigned roles, every second bringing them closer to the heart of the enemy's plan.

Alex: "We go in fast, keep it tight. We must be in and out before they know we're here."

He signaled, and they moved as one. The first layer of security was a network of cameras that scanned the perimeter, swiveling in a predictable pattern. Natalia's expertise came into play, looping the feeds to create brief windows of opportunity.

Natalia: "Now!"

They sprinted across the open ground, moving like phantoms. They reached the outer wall and paused as Max worked his magic, bypassing the thermal sensors with a device he had cobbled together from scraps and stolen tech.

Max: "We're clear. Let's move."

They slipped inside; the walls were lined with high-tech sensors, and the floors were pressure-sensitive, ready to alert the guards at the slightest deviation.

Alex: "We sweep the upper levels first."

They moved through the tiny hallways, twisting like a maze of hallways, advancing with military accuracy. Although guards were positioned at every intersection, the unit proceeded with trained simplicity, stealthily and effectively eliminating opponents. As they descended farther into the structure, the only noises were the muted thuds of people on the floor.

A high-pitched alert suddenly blared over the hallways. The boom sliced across the air like a dagger, causing the guards to panic. Alex's gaze flicked to Natalia, whose fingers rushed over the panel, frantically trying to turn off the alert.

Natalia: "It's a trap Viktor's set the system to trigger unauthorized access. We're exposed."

Alex: "We keep moving. No time to second-guess."

They pressed on, and the sound of guards rallying behind them got louder. The little tunnel expanded into a large, cavernous hall with high-tech machinery and foreign-symbol-marked containers. And in the middle of it all was Viktor Volkov, his shadow sharp against the flashing displays around him.

As they arrived, Viktor glanced up and started to smile twistedly. Highly armed mercenaries surrounded him, each one a monument to the force and savagery he commanded. But the serenity in his eyes unsettled Alex the sight of a guy precisely where he intended to be.

Viktor: "You made it, Alex. I was beginning to think you'd lost your nerve."

Alex stepped forward, his gun trained on Viktor, but he knew this confrontation was about more than bullets. It was a battle of minds, of wills, and neither man was willing to back down.

Alex: "It's over, Viktor. You're not getting out of here."

Viktor chuckled, the sound cold and hollow. He motioned to the guards, who fanned out, weapons ready.

Viktor: "You're so predictable, Alex. You are always playing the hero. But this isn't about winning or losing. This is about sending a message."

He took a step closer, his voice lowering to a dangerous whisper.

Viktor: "These people you're protecting the leaders, the institutions are all part of the same corrupt system. They use people like you and me, and when we're no longer useful, they discard us."

Alex tightened his grip on his weapon, his eyes never leaving Viktor. He had heard men like this before men with grudges, with vendettas. But Viktor's bitterness ran more profound. It was personal and drove every twisted action he took.

Alex: "You're just a terrorist hiding behind excuses. This isn't about justice. It's about your twisted ego."

Viktor's smile faded, replaced by a complex, dangerous glint. He moved swiftly, lunging at Alex with a knife in hand. The fight erupted in a blur of motion fists, knives, and raw, desperate violence. Alex dodged and countered, using every ounce of his training to keep Viktor at bay. They were evenly matched, exploiting the other's weaknesses and driven by something far more profound than the fight.

Viktor: "You don't understand, Alex. They ruined my life, and now I will ruin theirs."

Alex blocked a strike, twisting Viktor's arm and forcing the knife from his grip. The physical battle was only a fraction of the confrontation; the real fight was in their words and how each man sought to unnerve and outmaneuver the other. Viktor swung again, but Alex ducked, using the momentum to slam him against the wall.

Alex: "You're just another bully trying to rewrite the world in your image. But you're going to lose, Viktor. You're alone, and your delusions are going to cost you everything."

Viktor sneered, his breath ragged as he struggled against Alex's grip. It seemed like Viktor might break free for a moment, but Alex anticipated the move, twisting the knife out of Viktor's reach and throwing him to the ground. Viktor's eyes flickered with rage, but beneath that, there was something else fear. The realization that he was losing control and that his grand plan was unraveling.

The final blow was swift a calculated strike disarmed Viktor and left him gasping on the floor. Alex stood over him, breathless but victorious, his weapon trained on the man who had caused so much destruction.

Viktor: "You may have won this battle, Alex, but the war is far from over. There are others like me waiting for their turn."

Alex: "Let them come. You'll be the last."

The battle was far from over. Even as Alex subdued Viktor, the team was still engaged in a desperate fight against the remaining mercenaries. Max's voice crackled through the earpiece, strained and urgent.

Max: "Alex, we've got a problem. Natalia's hit bad. We need to get her out now."

Alex's heart dropped. The sound of gunfire and shouts filled his ears, drowning out his thoughts. He glanced over to where Natalia had taken cover. Viktor's remaining men were closing in, and they were outnumbered.

Alex: "Hold your positions! We're getting out of here."

But even as he said it, he knew the truth there wasn't enough time to do both. He could finish Viktor, or he could save Natalia. The decision clawed at him, a brutal reminder of what was at stake. He took a deep breath, weighing the impossible choice before him. In a flash of insight, Alex made his move. He signaled to Max to lay down cover fire while he darted towards Natalia. The bullets zipped past him, but he didn't hesitate. He reached Natalia's side, dragging her to safety with sheer determination.

Alex: "Stay with me, Natalia. I am not leaving you."

Alex drew Natalia behind a steel barrier and steadied her as best he could, using the anarchy to his advantage. Natalia's eyes opened, agony carved on his face, but there was also a flash of thankfulness there.

Natalia: "You didn't have to "

Alex: "We're a team. I'm not losing anyone today."

Alex turned back to where Viktor was struggling, frail but still rebellious, Natalia safe underneath. Alex had a mask of concentration and will on his face. He went quickly to provide Viktor with the last hit that knocked him out cold. Though the fight was done, Alex's decisions carried weight. Authorities swarming the site grabbed Viktor and his guys, and the sirens rang. Alex saw as they hauled Viktor away, cuffed. Still, Viktor's eyes had a terrible clarity, even in loss.

Viktor: "This isn't the end, Alex. You've won nothing. I'm just the beginning. There are others out there, just waiting for the right moment."

Alex: "Maybe. But today, you lose. And tomorrow, you'll be forgotten."

Viktor grinned coldly and far away. Though he had lost his fight, he adhered to his distorted views. Alex felt closure as the van doors shut, but also the residual anxiety held by Viktor's warning.

Though the immediate danger was past, the planet remained hostile. Alex understood this hard-fought and expensive triumph was only one chapter in a much bigger narrative as he gazed about at his squad, damaged but alive. Though the battle for a safer planet continued, they had salvaged the day.

Alex stayed quiet as the vehicle vanished beyond the horizon. Although they had won, they lost a lot. He saw in the features of his family his team the toll of their trip. Although this was not the end, it was a win sufficient for now.

Chapter Thirteen: The Aftermath

The mission was over, but the victory felt incomplete. Viktor had been captured, but during the chaos of transport, he had somehow managed to escape, slipping through the cracks and vanishing into the shadows. The team was left to grapple with the consequences of his disappearance and the toll the mission had taken on each of them.

Alex sat in silence, his thoughts distant. Natalia was resting on a nearby couch, her shoulder bandaged but still bleeding. She had taken a hit during the mission, which could have been fatal had Alex not prioritized her over everything else. Max worked at his console, his expression of grim focus as he monitored the city's feeds, searching desperately for any sign of Viktor.

Max: "Still nothing. He's gone. We'll keep tracking, but it's like he's vanished."

Alex nodded but said nothing. The reality of Viktor's escape weighed heavily on him. It was supposed to be over, but now it felt like they were back at square one. But Alex's gaze kept drifting back to Natalia. She was bruised, vulnerable in a way he hadn't seen her before, and it struck him just how close he'd come to losing her.

Max glanced over at Natalia, then back to Alex.

Max: "We got Emily though. She's in custody. Maybe she'll give us something useful."

His voice had no joy, only the acknowledgment of a battle half-won.

Natalia stirred, her eyes fluttering open. Despite the pain, she smiled faintly when she saw Alex watching over her. There was a silent conversation in that look a recognition of everything they had been through and the unspoken gratitude for Alex's decision during the fight.

Natalia: "You didn't have to save me."

Alex moved closer, his face a mix of concern and frustration.

Alex: "Yes, I did. You're part of this team, and I'm not about to let Viktor or anyone take that from me."

She looked at him, her eyes searching his.

Natalia: "You could have taken him down. But you chose to save me instead."

Alex sighed, leaning back against the wall, his expression softening.

Alex: "I made a choice. I'm not losing anyone else, Natalia not you, Max, or this team. Viktor's just one man. We'll get him again."

There was a quiet moment between them, filled with the weight of everything they had endured. Natalia reached out, her hand resting lightly on Alex's arm. It was a simple gesture, but it carried the unspoken bond that had grown between them a connection forged in fire and strengthened by trust.

Natalia: "Thank you."

They were more than just partners now; they were something closer, something that went beyond the mission. He had saved her, but in many ways, she had saved him too helping him find something to fight for that was more than just revenge.

***

Later, as the sun began to set, Alex found himself standing on a quiet street corner, staring at the worn memorial dedicated to those lost in past attacks. It was a place he hadn't visited in years, but today, it felt like the right place to be a reminder of what had driven him all this time and the people he had sworn to protect.

His thoughts drifted to his brother, whose memory had been the catalyst for everything. Alex knelt, placing his hand on the cold stone, tracing the etched names, and letting the emotions he had long buried rise. For so long, his brother's death had been the reason he fought, but now, it was about more than that.

Alex: "I'm sorry. I thought I had it under control. I thought taking Viktor down would end it, but it's never that simple."

He closed his eyes, letting the moment's silence fill the space between his thoughts. The anger that had fueled him for so long had finally begun to fade, replaced by something quieter but stronger a commitment to his brother's memory and the team that had become his new family.

He stood up, taking one last look at the memorial before turning away. The past would always be a part of him, but it no longer defined him. He had made mistakes, but today, he had made the right choice. He had chosen to protect the living and prioritize the people who stood by his side, and that decision gave him a sense of peace he hadn't known in years.

***

Back at headquarters, the team was already preparing for the next steps. Max coordinated with external agencies, sifting through surveillance footage and data to pick up Viktor's trail. Emily was being interrogated, and although she was still defiant, there was hope that she might eventually provide the information they needed.

Alex walked in, the weight of the day still on his shoulders but tempered by the sight of his team hard at work. They weren't giving up, and neither was he. Natalia was seated nearby, her arm in a sling, but her eyes were sharp, following every detail of the mission reports Max was pulling up.

Max: "Got some new intel. Seems like Viktor's people are already regrouping. We need to be ready this is far from over."

Alex: "We've got Emily. She's our best chance to figure out Viktor's next move. But we don't rely on luck. We keep pushing, keep digging. Viktor might have slipped away, but he's not invincible."

Natalia: "You've got a plan, don't you?"

Alex smirked, feeling a renewed sense of purpose.

Alex: "Always. We're not done. We will rebuild, refocus, and take this fight back to Viktor. And this time, we'll finish it."

The team nodded in agreement, each member feeling the same determination. They were bloodied but not beaten, and together, they would continue their fight against the shadows that threatened their world.

***

Max's console suddenly lit up with an incoming alert as the team continued strategizing. The room went silent as Max quickly scanned the data. His expression shifted from concentration to shock.

Max: "Alex, you need to see this."

Alex moved closer, his eyes narrowing at the screen. It was a live security feed from the transport route that had been used to transfer Emily to a secure facility. The footage showed a convoy under heavy attack vehicles overturned, guards scattered, and a familiar figure standing amidst the chaos.

It was Viktor. He wasn't fleeing. He was orchestrating a calculated assault to break Emily out. Natalia, watching from her seat, grimaced in pain but forced herself to stand.

Natalia: "He's not just escaping. He's regrouping. He's building something new."

The battle had shifted, and Viktor was no longer just a fugitive he was making a power play and wasn't alone.

Alex: "Get ready. We're going back out. This isn't over."

The screen flickered, showing Viktor's defiant grin as he freed Emily from her restraints. They were back in action, stronger than before, and the war Alex thought he had ended was only beginning.

Alex felt the familiar adrenaline rush as the room buzzed with frantic energy. Viktor had escaped, but this was no time to retreat. They had survived this long, and they would keep fighting together. Whatever Viktor had planned, Alex and his team would be ready to meet it head-on.

Alex turned to Natalia, their bond now unbreakable.

Alex: "We're in this, all of us. And we're not stopping until it's over."

Natalia: "Then let's finish what we started."

The fight was far from finished, and with Viktor back on the loose, a new chapter was about to unfold one that would test Alex and his team like never before.

About the Author

Maria Law draws inspiration from her personal journey of resilience and transformation. Her experiences with financial strain, rejection, and perseverance motivated her to try something new, and through her studies, she learned the value of patience and persistence.

Creating *"Operation Shadowstrike"* allowed her to escape daily worries and immerse herself in the world of fiction. After all, who doesn't love a little mystery in life? Through this espionage story, Maria hopes to offer readers a thrilling escape from everyday stress, or a perfect way to spend a rainy day immersed in action and excitement.

Life is never easy, but we all must find a way to fight through struggles and never give up on our dreams.

I hope you enjoy reading this espionage thriller, and who knows, perhaps more stories will follow once inspiration strikes again!

www.ingramcontent.com/pod-product-compliance
Lightning Source LLC
Chambersburg PA
CBHW051216120626
46547CB00013B/1379